1/7th Battalion THE ROYAL SCOTS

4th August 1914 to 11th November 1918

The Battalion formed part of the 156th Infantry Brigade
52nd (LOWLAND) DIVISION

By Lieut-Colonel W. Carmichael Peebles
D.S.O.

Leith 1920.

Published by
The Naval & Military Press Ltd
5 Riverside, Brambleside, Bellbrook
Industrial Estate, Uckfield, East Sussex,
TN22 1QQ England

Tel: +44 (0) 1825 749494

Fax: +44 (0) 1825 765701

www.naval-military-press.com

www.nmarchive.com

In reprinting in facsimile from the original, any imperfections are inevitably reproduced and the quality may fall short of modern type and cartographic standards.

1/7th BATTALION THE ROYAL SCOTS.

LEITH.

For some years before the outbreak of War the Seventh Battalion the Royal Scots was detailed for the Scottish Coast Defences and attached for training to the Lothian Infantry Brigade which at the time of Mobilisation was commanded by Brigadier General Horace Kays (H.L.I.) with Captain W.G. Neilson D.S.O. as Brigade Major.

On the 2nd August, 1914, the Battalion completed its two weeks of Annual Training and was dismissed. Two days later Mobilisation orders were received and all ranks were at once warned. Within 24 hours all paraded, passed their Medical Inspection and were detailed to their posts. One Company went to its Station at Blackness Castle, near Queensferry one took over the protection of Leith Docks; two were sent to Granton Harbour, and the rest were stationed in Leith Fort and in North Fort Street Public School, Leith.

On 12th August, 1914, the invitation came to Territorial Units to volunteer for Foreign Service. The Battalion returned all Officers and 85% of other Ranks. Meanwhile Home Defence Duties remained to be carried out.

Oct. 1914.
When the 3th Battalion The Royal Scots about 8 weeks later took over the Defence of Leith Fort and Docks from the 7th Battalion, the latter was posted to the Eastern Defences of Edinburgh from Duddingston to Seafield. At this period the personnel consisted of 24 Officers and 700 other Ranks under Command of Lieut. Colonel W. Carmichael, Peebles T.D., awith Captain J.G.P. Romanes. The Royal Scots, as Adjutant. The Battalion was quartered in the Marine Gardens and the Continental Chocolate Factory, Portobello Road, with piquets at Duddingston Village, Meadow Field Farm, The Warren, Craigentinny, Fillyside, and the Railway Line by the Beach at Seafield.

The formation of a Second Line Unit was taken in hand towards the end of September. Many of the old Officers of the Battalion, who had either transferred to the Territorial Force Reserve, or had retired from the 5th Volunteer Battalion The Royal Scots (this Unit's previous designation) were recalled or asked to rejoin. Amongst these were Captain H. Rose (later Temporary Lieut. Col. Commanding 3/7th Battalion The Royal Scots) Captains W.F. Harvey and J.H. Macdonald from the Territorial Force Reserve. Those of the 5th V.B.R.S. Officers included Captain C. Muirhead, (promoted later Temporary Lieut. Col. Commanding 2/7th Battalion The Royal Scots.

Captain H.A. Rose, (now Sir H. Arthur Rose) who later transferred to the 15th Battalion The Royal Scots, was promoted Temp. Lieut. Col. Commanding retiring with his rank after serving in France.

Captain W. Robertson appointed instructor in Machine Gunnery, St. Andrews.

Second Lieut. D.B. Allan appointed in the Field in Palestine Staff Captain 156th Infantry Brigade.

A nucleus of Officers and N.C. Os. to form a staff for the 2/7th Battalion (as it was later called) was detached/

detached from the 1/7th Battalion. Amongst the Officers were, Captain G.L. Watson, Lt. T. Clark (son of Sir John M. Clark Bart, M.B.E., V.D., a former Commanding Officer) Captain J.N. Bertram, Lt. L.Do. A. Mackenzie, Major & Qr Master A. Archibald R.S.M. D. Sutherland who afterwards became Lt. & Qr. Master.

Recruiting was now vigorously carried on. The task was a difficult one, however, owing to the demand for men for the New Armies raised under the scheme of the late Lord Kitchener and the requirements of the Regular Army. Notwithstanding a large number of new Officers and over 900 recruits were obtained, and Honorary Colonel R.G. Wardlaw Ramsay, V.D. (chairman of the Midlothian Territorial Force Association, which administered the Battalion) was gazetted Lieut. Col. and appointed to the Command.

The 1/7th Battalion was in every way complete and had added in 1913 an important Department in a V.A.D. detachment which was named after the Unit and received official recognition as No. 14 V.A.D. Midlothian. Mrs Arthur W. Sanderson, wife of Major Sanderson (Second in Command of the Battalion was first Commandant with 24 members, relatives and friends of the Officers, Mrs J. Douglas Dawson, wife of Captain J. Douglas Dawson, acting as Secretary. At the time the Detachment was formed there was no idea of foreign service for the Territorial Force. As has been stated the Battalion volunteered for service abroad, and members of the V.A.D. of the Battalion have nobly served in many Hospitals at home and abroad.

In order to complete the establishment to 1028 of all ranks two Companies complete with Officers, were drafted from the 8th Battalion H.L.I. early in December and towards the end of the year one half of the Battalion was moved from the Marine Gardens Portobello to the "Olympia", Leith Walk.

Jan. 1915

With the New Year came into force the new organisation known as the "Double Company System". Under this arrangement, "A" Company, under Command of Major J.D.L. Hamilton, absorbed "B" and "G" Companies. The two H.L.I. Companies under Captain I' Clark (H.L.I.) became "B" Company. "C" Company, under Captain J.D. Dawson absorbed "E" and "F" Companies and "D" Company, under Captain A.M. Mitchell, absorbed "A" and "D" Companies. The Seconds in Command of these Companies, in their order, were Captains J.M. Mitchell J.R. Torrance (H.L.I.) J.R. Peebles and A.J. Wightman respectively. Captain J. McD. Smith was appointed Intelligence Officer and Captain W.T. Ewing (being supernumerary) was appointed Assistant Intelligence Officer, Scottish Coast Defences.

In the early months of 1915, the general disposition of the Battalion remained unchanged though Companies relieved each other in their different posts from time to time, and a continuous training programme was systematically carried out, long route marches forming an important part of this training, 70 to 80 miles a week being a common occurrence.

Companies regularly relieved each other at Blackness Castle by route march, a distance of 17 miles. These marches were/

were much assisted by the Pipe Band under Sergeant Drummer J. Ross and Pipe Major J. Gear, while the Brass Band was under Band Master J. Wylie. A fine Set of Pipes and Drums was presented to the Battalion by Provost Malcolm Smith, the Town Council and Merchants of Leith.

The Pipe Band proceeded by the unfortunate train which was smashed on 22nd May, 1915, at Gretna, when all the personnel were either killed or seriously injured, while the members of the Brass Band became battalion stretcher bearers according to regulations.

1/7th Battalion was then freed from Coast Defence Duties for Foreign Service, and great were the rejoicings when the news came to hand.

April 1915.

On leaving Leith 24th April, to join the 52nd (Lowland) Division for overseas service, the Battalion was given a hearty send off by the townspeople, and at Central Station, Leith Provost Malcolm Smith and members of the Magistracy and Town Council presented each man with a suitable Gift. Proceeding to Larbert, the Battalion joined the 156th Infantry Brigade under Command of Brigadier General W. Scott Moncrieff, with Captain E.S. Girdwood The Sc.Rifles as Brig. Major, and encamped at Stenhousemuir. The other Infantry Units of the Brigade were the 4th Battalion The Royal Scots Lieut. Col. S.R. Dunn., the 7th Battalion Scottish Rifles Lieut. Col. J.B. Wilson, and the 8th Battalion Scottish Rifles Lieut. Col. H.M. Hannan, T.D.

After the inspection of the complete Unit by the Brigadier General Commanding a four days' period of leave began for 25% of all ranks at a time prior to embarkation for service abroad, hard and continuous training being carried out for those remaining. A second inspection was made by Major General G.G.A. Egerton, C.B. commanding 52nd (Lowland) Division, at Falkirk. The General expressed his satisfaction with the appearance of all ranks. Everything was now in readiness for the journey abroad, which, but for the stranding of H.M.T. "Aquitania" in the Mersey, would have begun somewhat sooner. As it was, the early hours of 22nd May saw the entraining of the Battalion for Liverpool, the port of embarkation; the Transport Section alone remained over till the afternoon. The first train, with the Commanding Officer and the whole of the Headquarters Staff, along with "A" and "D" Companies under the Command of Major J.D.L. Hamilton and Capt. A.M. Mitchell, respectively (a total of 15 Officers and 483 other Ranks) left at 3.45 a.m. while the remainder of the Battalion, under Major A.W. Sanderson followed in the second train which left Larbert two hours later. The Transport, under Lieut. A.O. Cushny, followed in the afternoon.

May 22nd 1915.

Few Leith Residents are likely soon to forget the anxious whisperings of that Spring afternoon, and the wave of dismay that later swept over the Burgh when it became known that the local Battalion on its way to the Front, had been involved in an appalling railway collision at Quentin's Hill Junction near Gretna. The next morning and afternoon brought further particulars of the disaster to the first train in which 3 Officers 29 N.Cos. and 182 men lost their lives, and as many more had sustained injuries.

The/

The morning was bright and clear, the run to Carlisle being made at high speed. At 6.45 the leading engine smashed into the tail of a local train drawn into a Siding, but with its rear carriages left projecting beyond the main line. The driver of the troop train at once applied the brakes on seeing the obstruction, but too late to avoid a collision, and the troop train was knocked off the rails and ran bumping along on the sleepers. This sent the whole train over on to the main down line, when a few seconds later the London Express, travelling North at full speed smashed into it, causing a fearful wreckage which immediately took fire, and the most appalling scenes were witnessed. The survivors at once got to work to help their stricken comrades and soon the whole neighbourhood was alarmed, and Motor Cars from near and far hastened to the spot with medical aid and other help. The kindness shown on all hands will never be forgotten, especially that of the people of Carlisle who gave such valuable assistance to the injured. Their hospitals were soon overflowing, but all who needed attention were quickly made as comfortable as possible. Their Majesties the King and Queen early sent sympathy and gifts to the Hospitals, and Lt. General Sir John Spencer Ewart K.C.B., Commanding in Chief, Scottish Command, hastened with his Staff to the spot. Mr G.W. Currie M.P. for Leith Burghs was indefaticable in his efforts to secure for the injured men and their dependants full recognition by the authorities of their claims for pensions and other allowances, while Col. Sir John M. Clark, Bart D.L. V.D., a former Commanding Officer made appoint of going round all the hospitals in Carlisle and neighbourhood visiting the injured, and calling on the distressed relatives at home.

The list of killed included the names of Major J.D.L. Hamilton a most efficient and popular officer Commanding "A" Company., Captain J.M. Mitchell his second in Command (brother of Capt. now Lt. Col. A. Maclaine Mitchell, D.S.O., Commanding 1/4th Battalion The Royal Scots) and Lieut. C.R. Salvesen (son of Col. J.T. Salvesen V.D. a former Commanding Officer) Machine Gun Officer while among the injured were Lieutenants W.R. Kermack and J.A. Young of "D" Company., Lieut. J.C. Bell and 2nd Lieuts. N.G. Salvesen and T.G. Clark of "A" Company.

The remnant who proceeded from Carlisle to Liverpool were but seven Officers and fifty-seven other Ranks. They were met, on arrival in the early hours of Sunday morning, by Brigadier General W. Scott Moncrieff, Commanding 156 Infantry Brigade the Brigade Staff, and by Major A.W. Sanderson, Second in Command, and the other Officers of the Battalion who, with their men had meantime reached Liverpool by making a detour round the scene of the disaster.

The Officers who had escaped injury were allowed to embark, but after conferring with the War Office, Major General G.G.A. Egerton O.B. G.O.C. 52nd (Lowland) Division returned all N.C.Os. and men to their homes in charge of Lt. N.C. Riddell.

This short account is given as it affected the Battalion at the moment, but a great deal more was done later by those at home in the tending of the injured. The funeral arrangements, followed by the erection of a beautiful memorial at Rosebank Cemetery, Leith, to the memory of those who/

who lost their lives was unveiled on the 12th May, 1916, by the Right Hon. The Earl of Rosebery K.G. K.T., Honorary Colonel of the Battalion in the presence of a large attendance of relatives and friends. Provost Malcolm Smith presided and was accompanied by the Magistrates and Town Council of Leith, General Sir John Spencer Ewart, K.C.B. Sir Robert K. Inches Lord Provost, of Edinburgh and members of the Edinburgh Town Council along with a large gathering of the Citizens of Leith and neighbourhood.

The service of dedication was conducted by the Honorary Chaplains of the Battalion., The Rev. Wm. Swan B.D. South Leith Parish Church, The Rev. James Harvey M.A. Lady Glenorchy's U.F. Church, Edinburgh and the Benediction was pronounced by the Right Rev. A. Wallace Williamson, D.D. Dean of the Thistle and Chapel Royal.

On the evening of Sunday 23rd May, H.M.T. "Empress of Britain" sailed from Liverpool carrying on board the six Officers and the half contingent of the Battalion which had travelled by the later train. The terrible and unnecessary loss of so many fine Officers, N.C.Os. and Men caused the greatest dismay amongst those on board and many regrets were heard on all sides of comrades missed whose places could never be filled.

During the voyage, which was pleasant and uneventful contributions were gathered from the Battalion with the result that £450 were cabled from Gibraltar to the Royal Scots Regimental Association for the immediate benefit of the Gretna disaster victims, their relatives and dependants. A further sum of £112 was sent by Divisional Headquarters, Brigade Headquarters and the three other Battalions aboard:- the 4th Royal Scots the 4th K.O.S.B. and the 7th Scottish Rifles. This practical and generous sympathy extended by the Headquarters, Staffs, and Sister Battalions was much appreciated by all Ranks of the Battalion.

June 1915

After a brief stay at Malta the Transport proceeded bound for Alexandria, which was reached on 3rd June. The Battalion disembarked on June 3rd and proceeded direct to Aboukir. There, the men had their first experience of marching on soft burning sands. On the other hand, there came a welcome opportunity of sea bathing situated as the Camp was near the Beach. Incidentially, it may be mentioned that it was here that 2nd Lieut. F.W. Thomson rushing into the water without divesting himself of clothes, gallantly swam out a considerable distance and rescued a man from drowning.

All ranks had suffered considerably from the unaccustomed roasting weather conditions when the order arrived on 8th June to re-embark at Alexandria.

Passage to Mudros Bay, through the sunny Grecian Archipelago, was a most interesting experience to all on board; nor was the interest lessened when the Bay itself, with its splendid anchorage, was reached on Friday, 11th June, 1915 and found to be dotted all over with ships of various kinds including British and French men of War.

Soon/

Soon the stirring news arrived that the Battalion would proceed next day to the Peninsula of Gallipoli, and presently H.M.T. "Carron" came along side when the Battalion and all Brigade Stores were put aboard. It was but a five hours' sail to Cape Helles, which was reached at 7 p.m., while daylight still lasted, and before the operation of landing troops and stores could proceed, so that the vessel had to cruise about well out of sight and of shell range. At night-fall that operation commenced and owing to both darkness and the choppy sea it was no easy affair. The Trawlers, three in number, received the Troops and Stores, and in the small hours the landing began. In the early hours of Sunday 13th June, the first Trawler, with four Officers and a Platoon, made for V. Beach, followed shortly afterwards by another, while the last, with the remainder of the Battalion on board, steered for W. Beach, otherwise known as Lancashire landing.

The getting ashore of the Stores in the dark was a strenuous business, as may well be imagined, when it is remembered that at any moment the progress of the work could have been impeded by the attentions of enemy artillery. All went off, however, without a hitch, the Battalion and Stores being landed with only two casualties.

The Troops that had landed by the "River Clyde" on V. Beach marched off to their Camp nearly two miles from the South end of the Peninsula, and arriving before daylight at once dug themselves in. They were joined later by those who went ashore at Lancashire landing.

It was not intended to push the men right away into the fighting line, so that while Officers and Parties of N.C.Os. visited sections of the firing line to familiarise themselves with the conditions, the Battalion itself was for a time occupied mainly with digging and construction work, occasionally under shell fire, proceeding to the "ESKI" line on 19th June in Divisional Reserve to 29th Division. Some few casualties were sustained during this period, as no part of the Peninsula was secure from artillery bombardment, and the enemy maintained throughout the practice of unaimed rifle fire over areas where our men were employed in cutting communication trenches. All Ranks soon got accustomed to the shelling and rifle fire, and paid little heed to either.

There was one condition of life in the Campaigns both in Gallipoli and Egypt the Troops never got used to viz: the awful plague of flies the dust and fine sand and the great want of water.

The myriads of flies especially during the heat of the day made life almost unbearable being a constant source of annoyance and irritation as well as being a real danger to health. A great deal of the illness from which the troops suffered so much was traced to this cause. The flies grew in numbers larger and ever larger especially on the Peninsula owing to the contracted area of the occupied territory used as it was by both sides for the burial of the dead-men and animals and being the dumping ground for refuse which could not be burned.

No contrivance was really successful in lessening their intolerable persistence in covering the person whether asleep/

asleep or awake or seemed of the slightest use and the difficulties with the food may be best left to the imagination.

The fine dust on the Peninsula and the penetrating sand of the desert rose in great clouds with the slightest wind and filled every pore. Nothing could keep it out.

The want of water in these parched regions for so large a body of troops was always a serious problem, more important even that the want of food. That both difficulties were overcome was due to the constant energy of the Army Service Corps and The Royal Engineers, and the heroic endurance of the men.

This period of work was followed by a short rest in the bivouac area, and then on Sunday 27th June came the Intelligence that the Battalion was to join in an attack the following day.

The effective strength at this time was 18 Officers and 450 men.

SECTION II.

June 28th 1915

The line of Turkish Defences to be attacked included a strongly fortified ridge dominating a depression known as " Gully Ravine".

The 156th was the first Infantry Brigade of the 52nd (Lowland) Division to arrive on Gallipoli. On 28th June it was attached to the 29th Division and was ordered to attack the trench system immediately East of the Ravine. The attack was timed to begin at 11 a.m., and was part of a general advance of the British line on the left sector of the Peninsula. The Brigade was disposed with 1/8th Scottish Rifles on the right, 1/7th Battalion The Royal Scots in the centre, and 1/4th Battalion The Royal Scots on the left, while the 1/7th Scottish Rifles formed Brigade Reserve.

The Railway Disaster at Gretna had reduced the 7th R.S. Battalion to two Companies, of these "C" Company was sent into the line, holding a front of 150 yards, and was detailed to lead in the assault. Captain J.D. Dawson Commanded with Captain J.R. Peebles Second in Command the other Officers being Lts. E.J. Thomson and R.M. Galloway, and 2nd Lts. F.W. Thomson D. Lyell and G. Haws while "B" Company (H.L.I. attached) was to follow in immediate support. "B" Company (H.L.I.) was Commanded by Captain D. Clark with Captain J.R. Torrance Second in Command, the other Officers being Lts. J. Ballantyne and 2nd Lt. T. McClelland LT. A.S. Elliot (H.L.I.) became Machine Gun Officer on the death of Lt. C.R. Salvesen at Gretna with 2nd Lt. W.C. Mc Geachin (H.L.I.) as his Assistant. Major A.W. Sanderson was in Command of the assault.

The artillery bombardment of the enemy front line and reserve trenches began at 9 a.m. The Turks at once replied and the most appalling noise prevailed. Our men were having their first experience of the crash and din of a battle-field. To/

To raise one's head above the parapet had become unhealthy, and such casualties, as were sustained at this period were the result of the searching artillery fire directed against our front line and support trenches. Promptly at 11 a.m., Captain Dawson gave the Command to attack, and like one man, Officers and Men sprang over the top and raced for the Turkish line. A few seconds later Capt. Torrance led his support in the same way, and Capt. Clark immediately followed with the remaining two platoons of "B" Company Several casualties occurred within a few yards of our own line, but the majority of the men got well forward and captured the first line, the Turks retiring by the flanks. The attacking waves had now closed up, and the second rush was made to the final objective, which was likewise captured. During the second rush a large number of Officers and Men were either killed or wounded. Major Sanderson and several others were killed half way across the open; Captain Dawson and Lt. E.J. Thomson on reaching the final trench. Here it was found that of those taking part in the attack only three Officers, Lt. Haws and 2nd Lts. Lyell and McClelland, with 80 other Ranks were unwounded. These Officers at once organised the men and proceeded with the consolidation of the line. A large number of Turks were accounted for in this advance, which was extended on the left by the 1/4th Battalion The Royal Scots, and to some extent on the right by the 1/8th Scottish Rifles, and a platoon of the 1/7th Scottish Rifles sent up from the reserve to fill up a gap on the right of the 1/7th Battalion The Royal Scots, Unfortunately, the 1/8th Scottish Rifles could not get completely forward on the right, as the position was held by the Turks with a veritable nest of machine guns, and remained in the Turkish hands until the evacuation. Brigadier General W. Scott Moncrieff was killed while personally leading forward the reserve Companies of the 1/7th Scottish Rifles to assist the right flank of the attack. His death was much regretted by all who remained after that terrible day. The attack had succeeded, but at heavy cost. Officers of the Battalion killed were:-

Major A.W. Sanderson, Second in Command
Captain J.D. Dawson, Commanding "C: Coy
Lieut. E.J. Thomson, A.S. Elliot, and
2nd Lts F.W. Thomson,

  Wounded:-
Captains A.J. Wightman, J.R. Torrance, and
Lieut. J. Ballantyne

  Died of Wounds:-
Captain D. Clark. Commanding "B" Coy

  Missing:-
Captain J.R. Peebles and Lt. R.M. Galloway

Of other Ranks there were:-

Killed ... 7
Wounded ...114
Missing ...109

During the attack our Machine Guns, Commanded by Lt. A.S. Elliot (8th H.L.I.) did excellent service with crossfire in keeping down enemy heads, and thus preventing the infliction of even greater loss to our side. Unfortunately/

Unfortunately Lt. Elliot was killed about 2 p.m. while observing the fire of the guns. 2nd Lt. W.C. McGeachin then took over command of the machine Guns. When the position had been taken Captain A.J. Wightman endeavoured to run out a telephone wire and with Sergt. Rosie he led four signallers carrying cables and instruments towards the captured trench. In the course of this brave attempt Sergt. Rosie was killed and Capt. Wightman wounded, though the latter carried on till every man was knocked out, and he himself was again wounded and fell. He lay out all day and most of the night was hit a third time, but recovered sufficiently to crawl into our lines towards dawn next wmorning. For this gallant action he was awarded the Military Cross. The Battalion had lost all its Signal Section at Gretna, and this constituted a serious handicap, but Captain Wightman and the men who were chosen to start a new Section had devoted the whole of their time on the voyage out to acquiring the use of Morse Code and a general knowledge of signalling work. Their great performance was, therefore, all the more creditable.

      Privates No. 7101 A. Hind and No. 7259 J. McIntyre both H.L.I. men did magnificent work in carrying out ammunition across the fire swept Zone, and were mentioned in "Dispatches", Private McIntyre receiving besides the D.C.M. Private Hind was killed.

      Lt. Col. J. Mill V.D., R.A.M.C. regardless of personal danger established his Dressing Station close up to the Firing Line from which the advance was made, and from an early stage was busy at his post. He carried on invaluable work during the whole day and well into the night, promptly dressing and succouring the wounded prior to their evacuation down the long communication trenches and mule track to the advanced stations of the Field Ambulance.

      The Quarter-master Capt. G. Gordon Weir displayed great initiative and determination in getting forward, under heavy shell fire, supplies of small arms, ammunition and water. Owing to the heat conditions the latter was an immense boon to all partioularly to the wounded.

      Writing after the action 2nd Lieut. David Lyell gave an account of his experience:-

> "I was standing with my eye on my watch, and just on 11 was about to give the word to advance when from the right I saw a movement, so shouted "Come on", and over the parapet the whole Company went like one man We had about 100 yards to go to the first trench to take that, and then about 250 yards to the next one. As soon as we started the Turkish artillery opened on us a perfect rain of shrapnel, and some machine guns turned on us from somewhere. The first trench took some taking I know I loosed off all six chambers of my revolver, then the Turks bolted and then we went to the second trench still under this awful fire. The Turks didn't wait for us there at all, but all flew. The chief thing I remember about the charge was the awful noise. After we got to the second trench we had rather an anxious time as only three subalterns of the 7th got there, and we had all,the responsibility of putting the trench into a state of defence. Fortunately, the Turks had got such a fright that they did not attack/

attack again till after dark. Poor Dawson and Jim Thomson were both killed just at the parapet of the second trench."

In the words of an eye-witness - as mentioned in

"The Royal Scots", by Lawrence Weaver:-

"At 10.30 all the guns in the place were pouring forth, assisted by battleships, and the Turks were replying with all they had. The din was terrific, and words cannot possibly describe it. Promptly at 11 a.m. the bayonet charge started. The 7th Royal Scots under Captain Dawson Captain Peebles, and five subs, climbed over the firing line parapet, and advanced in great style, cheering and yelling. A moment later the second line, under Captain Torrance and Lieutenant Ballantyne, followed and a moment after that, the third line, under Captain Clark, tore after them. The first and second lines captured the first Turkish trench, lay down and opened rapid fire. When the third line got forward, they rose and advanced with us, and we took the second trench with another wild rush..........
We at once threw up barricades, and put on two good shots, in case Mr. Turk tried to visit us, but he did not do so. Reinforcements arrived, and we were all right then and started to consolidate our position by turning the Turkish trench about turn, and making it a fire trench against them. At midnight Regulars came in and relieved us for a sleep .... During the afternoon the Turks endeavoured to mass and get forward with a counter-attack, but what with rapid fire and machine guns we simply mowed them down in hundreds Their losses must have been enormous. Through the ravine, on our immediate left, their dead bodies were lying piled in thick and confused heaps. Our advance had driven them out of two elaborate trenches and out of this ravine which looks as if it had been a kind of Headquarters for them".

About 8 o'clock in the evening the Turks counter-attacked, but were swept back with heavy loss, and then at 9.30 came the welcome news of relief. This was effected by the Hants, Regiment and completed by 3 o'clock in the morning when our men returned to Camp for rest which lasted but a few hours as cleaning up and salvage duties were required in the line.

Thus the Gretna Disaster and the result of the first action reduced the strength of the Battalion to 7 Officers and 217 other Ranks. This in a period of five weeks, which included over three weeks' voyage out. The Battalion had left Larbert on 22nd May at full strength, viz. 31 Officers and 997 other Ranks.

To those remaining the loss of so many fine comrades was much felt. All had worked since mobilisation to fit themselves for the stern work ahead, and the Battalion, on leaving home, was considered by all who came in contact with it, to be in a high state of efficiency

Of the Officers killed, Major A.W. Sanderson, second in Command was entitled to the Territorial Decoration (for over 20 years' service) a highly efficient Officer, fully qualified for Command of the Battalion and most popular with all ranks. Captain J.D. Dawson and Captain/

J.R. Peebles had many years of volunteer and Territorial Service to their credit. Lieutenants E.J. Thomson and R.M. Galloway, and 2nd Lieutenant F.W. Thomson had shown exceptional interest and keenness in all their work and had endeared themselves to hthe Officers and to their men. All were sadly missed.

Captain D. Clark and 2nd Lieutenant A.S. Elliot 1/8th H.L.I. since being attached to this Battalion at the end of 1914, had proved their ability and become great favourites with all Ranks

Of the N.C.Os. and men the same may be said. They were all tried comrades who had been with the Battalion or with the 1/8th H.L.I. for many years and were of the finest type of Territorial soldier. Keen and interested in their work, with a fine esprit de corps, most anxious to do their duty to King and Country, they made the supreme sacrifice, all honour to them.

As Leiut. Col. S.R. Dunn and all senor Officers of the 4th had been either killed or wounded in the attack on 28th June, the 1/4th Battalion (5 Officers and 519 other Ranks) were attached to the 1/7th Royal Scots to form the Royal Scots Battalion under the Command of Lieutenant Colonel Peebles, 7th Royal Scots. Lieutenant Colonel P.C. Palin 29th Indian Brigade now took over Command of the Brigade.

July 1915

The next move of the Brigade was to Ghurka Bluff on 3rd July where it relieved the Indian Brigade. The Royal Scots composite Battalion held the front line with the 1/7th and 1/8th Scottish Rifles, also formed into a single composite unit, in reserve. After six days the Units relieved each other.

The line was comparatively quiet during the few days' occupation, but the driven sand and want of water were very trying. The Battalion's stay in the front line was marked by an unusual incident which occurred on 7th July. About 4 o'clock that morning the Turks displayed a White Flag, and on this being answered by a Khaki Handkerchief tied to a stick a Turkish Officer left his Trench and advanced towards our lines. After proceeding a few paces he was given the order to halt. and Colonel Peebles, accompanied by an orderly, went out to meet him. The Turkish Officer's message was to deliver a letter to the Commander-in-Chief of the Brittish Army. After arranging for an answer to be returned as soon as possible both parties turned back to their Trenches, and the front lines resumed their normal aspect. In the afternoon Colonel Palin arrived in person, with an interpreter, and after due formalities were exchanged the latter went out with the answer. It was generally believed that the object of the Turks was to obtain as armistice for the burial of their dead, a large number, (about 400) of whom were lying out in front of our trenches as a result of the last counter-attack.

After this spell at Ghurka Bluff the Brigade moved back to the Rest Camp, but was only there one day when orders were received to move at 3 a.m. before dawn on 12th July to Backhouse Post a distance of over two miles from the/

the scene of the attack on 28th June and behind the right sector of the British line across the Peninsula. Here the Brigade was to lie in divisional reserve to the 155th and the 157th Brigades. The Royal Scots Battalion, however, was at once thrown into the line, two Companies of the 4th Royal Scots being sent to fill up a gap that existed between the British and French Fronts, the remaining Company (The 7th Royal Scots) being ordered to attack a Turkish position. On the way there Lieutenant Haws, the Officer in charge of the 7th Royal Scots Company was wounded and the Command devolved upon 2nd Lieutenant D. Lyell. After working its way along the communication trenches the Company made a desperate charge and completely routed the enemy. To the deep regret of all 2nd Lieutenant Lyell was killed while engaged in the work of consolidating the newly captured position. 2nd Lieut. Lyell showed great skill and resource in handling his men. A son of Col. David Lyell D.L.V.D., Secretary of the Midlothian Territorial Association which administers the Battalion, 2nd Lieut. Lyell joined the Battalion immediately on the outbreak of War. His sterling qualities soon made him a great favourite with all ranks. His death was much lamented. 2nd Lieut. T. McClelland, the only remaining Officer, successfully accomplished this task. The Company now found itself in advance of the front line held by the 5th King's Own Scottish Borderers, with the 4th and 5th Royal Scots Fusiliers to their right; but later the Scottish Rifles continued the line occupied by the 7th Royal Scots Company now supported by the Companies of the 4th Royal Scots, and all held to the positions taken against successive counter-attacks. On the day following the capture of the position there occurred an incident worth mentioning as showing the resourcefulness of our men. The Machine-gun Section had been kept in reserve and was ordered to prepare to move. The Sergeant, being at the moment on fatigue duty, was not present when the order arrived., but after waiting some time without further instructions one party of six privates went off with a gun to the front line. Noticing an attack develop on the front of the 7th H.L.I., the Section at once came to the support, and drove the Turks out of a trench performing great execution. They remained at their position till the next morning, when they were joined by the other gun and the remainder of the personnel till orders were received to rejoin Headquarters at the old French Lines. The Battalion was relieved on 14th July by the Chatham Battalion Royal Naval Division, when it moved into reserve at the ESKI Trench Line which ran right across the Peninsula, and a couple of days later it reached Rest Camp in Corps Reserve. In connection with the action 12th to 15th July, Lieut. Col. W.C. Peebles and Lieut. T. McClelland were mentioned in Sir Ian Hamilton's Dispatch.

The casualties suffered by the Royal Scots Battalion during the action were:-

1/4th Battalion The Royal Scots:-
    Officers Nil, ...   Other Ranks Killed 18
                                               " Wounded   47
                                               " Missing   9

1/7th Battalion The Royal Scots:-
    Officers, Killed   1 .... Other Ranks Killed 13
      " Wounded,   1   " Wounded   29
                                               " Missing   9

The strength of the Battalion then was :-
1/4th Royal Scots ... Officers 5, Other Ranks,   455
1/7th Royal Scots ... Officers 5, Other Ranks   169

SECTION III.

From now to the end of July the only events of outstanding importance for the Battalion was the appointment of Brig. Gen. L.C. Koe to the Command of the Brigade, and the loss of the services of Lieut. Col. James Mill, V.D. R.A.M.C. the Battalion Medical Officer, to hospital owing to illness. For his splendid work he was awarded the Croix de Guerre. Lieut. Col. Mill was followed by several Medical Officers amongst others, Capt. G. Hunter, R.A.M.C. 1/3rd Lowland Field Ambulance Lieut. E.M. Bruce Payne, R.A.M.C. Lieut. R. Lennie R.A.M.C. 1/1st L.F.A. Captain A.W. Sutherland R.A.M.C. 1/1st L.F.A. Captain J.C. Bell R.A.M.C. who was evacuated sick after a short service with the Battalion and died in Alexandria Hospital Captain P.J. Moir, R.A.M.C. 1/1st L.F.A.

Aug. 1915

The 6th and 7th August, 1915 will be remembered for the landing at Suvla Bay, and the vigorous feints at Helles to divert the Turks attention.

The Battalion, occupied in succession, various positions in the front and reserve lines with periods at Rest Camp in Divisional or Corps Reserve. On 10th August a much needed addition to the strength of Officers was made by the arrival of Captain A.M. Mitchell, Lieut. W.R. Kermack and Lieut. N.C. Riddell, after recovering from the effects of their injuries at Gretna. Col. A. Young V.D. reached the Peninsula on the following day and took over Command of the 4th Royal Scots. The two Scottish Rifle Battalions remained an amalgamated Unit. On 17th August, the Battalion took over a portion of the Line to the West of the "Vineyard" from the 6th H.L.I. On 18th August, the 7th Royal Scots received a further accession to the strength of Officers when Lieut. N.W. Stewart A.N. Rogers, W.L. Innes 2nd Lieuts. M. Smith G. Pender J.E. Flett and R. Cairns disembarked and joined the Unit. The last named unfortunately was invalided to hospital soon after landing. During all this period there was comparative quiet along the Front. Bombing saps were constructed from which bombs might be thrown by hand or catapult at enemy strong points situated here and there only 30 to 40 yards away. Sniping was carried on, and measures were adopted to circumvent enemy snipers who were endeavouring to make certain of our communications, and Krithia Nullah, in particular, unsafe to use, and all were under arms daily at "stand to". For the benefit of those who are unacquainted with military terms it may be stated that "stand to" usually covers two periods of the day, the hour before dawn and the hour after sunset. These are generally considered to be suitable occasions for a raid or attack in force and so the trenches are fully manned and remain so until the danger period is supposed to be past. Trained observers and listening posts are then stationed forward all along the Line, while the remainder of the garrison "stand down" and either rest or proceed with such work as may locally be required. An attack at these times is generally in the nature of a surprise, and when such takes place at dawn and a hostile trench is occupied the work of consolidation, i.e. reversing the parapet, proceeds in daylight, the enemy being held off by fire while communication trenches leading forward are blocked and when a suitable opportunity arrives, wire entanglements are placed out in front. If, on the other hand, the attack is carried out as it is growing dark/

dark, advantage is taken of the temporary confusion in the enemy lines to complete consolidation as far as possible before he has recovered and collected sufficient reserves to deliver a counter-attack.

Sept. 1915

3rd September stands out as as an important date in the Battalion records, for on that day a suitable addition was made to the Ranks by the arrival of a large draft, known thereafter as "THE FIVE HUNDRED DRAFT". The draft consisting of the following Officers and 440 other Ranks, was under the Command of Captain W.T. Ewing, 7th Royal Scots and the other Officers were Captains J. Sommerville and J.Scott (1/8th H.L.I.), Lieuts.J.C. Bell J.A. Young, the two last named having recovered from their injuries at Gretna J.B. Greenshieks, 2nd Lieuts D.B. Allan, N.S. Pringle Pattison, 7th Royal Scots, also 32nd Lieuts. U.A. Currie T.B. Forrest, J. Scott and D. Brown (1/8th H.L.I.) the latter Officer after a week in the Line was evacuated to hospital and died on board the Hospital Ship during the passage home.

About the middle of September rain fell for the first time, making the soil very greasy and movement difficult. Yet it was as nothing compared to the tropical downpours that came later and flooded many of the trenches. It was about this time that the Turks began to use Trench Mortars. Our own men, with Trench Mortars, had been making some good practice at a strongly traversed trench which the enemy held between the East and West Krithia Nullahs. The Turks fired a shell 9 inches long by 3 inches in diameter called a "Broom Stick" Bomb serrated to break up into about one hundred pieces, the interior being filled with shrapnel bullets half-an-inch in diameter, bits of old iron nails, etc. This projectile had a broom stick four feet long fitted at the end from which it took its name. It did not apparently work much damage,

On 27th September at a pre-arranged hour a great cheer was raised along the whole British Front in honour of the victory at Loos in France, and proclamations inserted in bottles, were flung into the Turkish Trenches. Believing that an advance against their lines was in contemplation the Turks opened rapid fire, wasting thousands of rounds. Of this little incident an annonymous writer penned the following verses:-

"With faces flushed and eyes like wine
  The men sat mute along the line,
    And some polemical design
      Was palpably in view.
A flare soared sudden through the murk
  They turned unflinching towards the Turk,
    And shouted all they knew.

No ordered cheer, but each man cried,
  The sound on which he most relied,
    Or just invoked the "Soccer" side,
      Of which he once was proud,
A milk-man happily "milk-o'ed",
  Myself I simply said "Well rowed"
    But said it very loud.

A wilder din you will not meet,
It hit the hills, it shocked the Fleet,
And many a brave heart dropped a beat,
   To hear the hideous choir,
While the pale Turk, with lips tight set,
   Peered out across the parapet,
   And opened rapid fire.

For it was clear the Christian Cur,
   Intended something sinister,
And Pashas hastened to confer,
   On that hypotheses
Stout souls, they felt prepared to cope
   With stratageme within their scope,
   But Allah what was this.

For down the lines the Faithful heard,
   And had no notion what occurred,
But plied their triggers undeterred,
   By trifles such as that,
From sea to sea the tumult spread
Nor could a single man have said,
   What he was shouting at.

Then spoke the guns, and gave it hot,
   To the offensive choric spot,
Where we who shrank from being shot,
   Had long since ceased to be,
   And even "Asiatic Anne,"
Disgorged a bolt of monstrous plan,
   Which fell into the sea,

I would that night Byzantium,
Had been at hand to hear the hum,
   And count the cost a fearful sum,
   of so much S. A. A.
For no one but the Moslem knows,
The way the ammunition goes,
   When he is on his day,

And what of those whose mad caprice
Had frightened half the Chersonese;
Did they repentant know no peace,
And when at dawn there crept,
A sheepish hush, o'er crag and glen,
Pray that they might be better men?
Instead of that they slept.

And a despatch in pleasing wise,
Spoke of a daring enterprise,
"Against some enemy supplies",
Adding this tragic note:-
The casualties of the force,
Were sixty men extremely hoarse,
And one severe sore throat".

   The usual repair of trenches, attention to loopholes and strengthening of barbed wire defences went on during this period without any incident of importance taking place, although a good deal of mining and countermining was carried on by both sides.

   Early /

Oct 1915

Early in October we began to turn our attention to a Turkish trench running along the West Krithia Nullah and were successful in our first bombardment with catapults. A scheme was presently drawn up for the attack and capture of this position, and was ready to be put into effect when the Battalion was relieved by the 7th Highland Light Infantry. After a week's rest the Battalion took over a portion of the Line at Achi Baba Nullah on the right of the "Vineyard". Soon afterwards the 1/1st Lanarkshire Yeomanry Battalion (dismounted) under the Command of Lt. Col. Lord Dunglas which had just arrived out were attached. They were a fine body of men and great good feeling very soon existed between the Units. Trench work must have proved a very slow and wearisome game to men who had been trained to rapid movement by bounds from one position to another. The enemy were active during this period, paying much attention to one of ourBombing Stations, strengthening his own Line, revetting trenches, making overhead cover and running out barbed wire. It was our business to interrupt, as far as possible, the work of these parties either by bombing them or directing rifle and machine-gun fire on them. Some very good practice was made from a distant point by means of telescopic rifles used by the Adjutant. Captain J.G.P. Romanes and Lieut. U.A. Currie and J.B. Greenshields. The Turks, however, renewed their attempts upon F. 13, our pet bomb station, and were so annoyed at being dispersed by our rapid fire and bombs that they bombarded the Station and kept up heavy sniping, finally calling down punishment from our Monitors which bombarded two of their large redoubts, and one was glad the Turks had no Monitors wherewith to reply. Their bombardment of F.13 continued though they failed to inflict a single casualty. L/Corporal Kelly and Private Watson displayed great courage and endurance, remaining at their posts, one observing with a periscope and the other ready with a periscopic rifle in case the enemy ventured to advance. Failing with their bombardment the Turks returned to the use of bombs but did not succeed in reaching their objective, while out bombs landed repeatedly on their shelters. The next spell in the firing line was somewhat more exciting.

Nov. 1915

On 7th November, the Battalion, with the 4th Royal Scots again attached (on Col. A. Young going to hospital) and the 1/1st Ayrshire Yeomanry (Col. J. Boswell) relieved the 4th King's Own Scottish Borderers at Krithia Nullahs on a frontage of 500 yards. On 13th November Captain J.G.P. Romanes went to hospital, being succeeded by 2nd Lt. U.A. Currie as Acting Adjutant. The Turks had greatly strengthened their position by wire entanglements since last we were on this front. For some days the usual trench garrison duties were carried out, but shortly before 15th November the 156th Infantry Brigade prepared to attack trenches on the East side of East Krithia Nullah by the Scottish Rifles Battalion with No. 2 and No. 4 Companies 1/7th Royal Scots attached, and, on the West side of West Krithia Nullah by the Royal Scots Battalion less two companies. The signal for the attack, which was successfully carried out on 15th November at 3 o'clock in the afternoon was the springing of two mines, one under a Turkish Bomb Station (in Trench H.11 A.; dealt with by 1/7th Royal Scots, and the other just West of the "Vineyard" by the Scottish Rifles. The explosions were tremendous, the ground in the whole vicinity being shaken/

shaken, and while the dust and debris were still in the air, our Bombers, led by Lt. J. Scott (1/8th H.L.I.) and Sergt. T. Berry instructed by Lieut. U.A. Currie, Battalion Bombing Officer, tore through a gap that had been prepared under the advanced barricades and rushed up to the top of H.11.A. The attack was a complete success, as numbers of the enemy left their dug-outs to see what was happening and were at once disposed of. In the melee a huge Turk, emerging from a dug-out, took aim from behind at Lt. Scott with his rifle, fortunately, the rifle jammed and before the Turk could gain control of it he was shot by Corporal Kelly, who thus saved his officer's life. Proceeding down a cross-trench the attackers found the Turks sitting in niches with their bayonets just appearing above the trench; after throwing a few bombs among them, our men having gone beyond their objective retired a few yeards and erected sandbag barricades to hold up any Turks who might attempt to return. A tremendous amount of digging was required to clear the captured trench H.11.A which had been practically filled in by the Mine Explosion and unfortunately during the progress of this work Lt. J.E. Flett was killed whilst directing a digging party from the top of the crater. Lt. Flett's death was a great loss to the Battalion, as he has endeared himself to all ranks. The amount od digging required to clear a passage and re-establish communication may be imagined when it is realised that it occupied the whole of No. 1 Company under Captain A.M. Mitchell and Lt. D.B. Allan from 3 o'clock on 15th November until 6 o'clock the following, eveningz Valuable assistance was rendered in this work by Lance Corporal J. Priestly 2/1st Lowland Field Company R.E. Corporal Priestly was killed at his post on the second day of the attack. Lieut. Allan carried on the work immediately after Lt. Flett had fallen, and for his bravery andtenacity was awarded the Military Cross.

Lt. Scott's party of bombers were cut off from their comrades for over two hours; Sergt Berry had led his party down a small gap overlooking the Nullah, which had been a regular means of communication for the Turks, and a barricade was built at the exit by the Cliff face. This sap was afterwards known as "Berry's Sap". The sergeant and his party were completely cut off from the rest of the trench for over six hours until the accumulation of earth caused by the explosion had been cleared away. Sergt. Berry was unfortunately killed by a sniper next morning while he was directing operations. For his splendid services he was specially mentioned in Dispatches. Over 10.000 sandbags were used on the parapets, in the course of the work of consolidation 2000 of these having been filled and laid in readiness before the attack, and passed from man to man placed at yard intervals along the trench. While the consolidation proceeded both sides kept up heavy rifle and machine-gun fire, and the trench was enfiladed by the enemy with shrapnel fire. This trench was afterwards known as "Roseberry Street" after Lord Roseberry, Hon. Colonel of the Battalion. While it was being strengthened another trench was dug, run out from one of our Bomb Stations (No.9) to about the centre of it, and communication established by 8 o'clock of the second evening. This new trench, afterwards known as "Forrest Road", was, for the greater part, dug by the 4th Royal Scots (whose Head-quarters are in Forrest Road, Edinburgh) It was over 100 yards/

yards long, led through heavy soil and much of the work fell to be done at night in the open. It was later discovered that the capture included an enemy mine-shaft, which led below our No. 9 Bomb Station, and was within two hours of completion. The charge indeed was ready to place in position. Furthmore, a second shaft was discovered leading under the Station, from which our advance was made. It started from the enemy bomb station which we exploded, and great surprise was occasioned amongst those busy with the work of consolidation when they heard a voice from beneath say in a strange tongue "Taal C'hena" (Come here). Eventually the Turk was extricated from the debris none the worse of his two days' internment, but very hungry. Of these enemy mine-shafts which were captured, the first named was a fine peice of work. It was lined throughout with wood, and its value to the Turks was shown by the endeavours they made all through the night and during the next day to recapture it, small parties creeping or rushing forward at intervals towards our barricades. These parties were, as a rule, bombed or shot down. A determined effort was made at 8 o'clock of the second evening when a party crept up from the low ground at the edge of the cliff and rushed our barricade. They succeeded in gaining a footing, but were at once driven out by bombs and bayonet, our Bombers being led by Lieut. J.B. Greenshields 7th Royal Scots, and Lieut. J.A. Neilson 1/1st Ayrshire Yeomanry. The latter officer was wounded by a shrapnel bullet. After this failure, the Turks gave little further trouble. The surprise nature of the attack and the vigour with which it was conducted were, no doubt, responsible for the comparatively short list of casualties occurring in the Unit. - One Officer killed, Lt. Flett, one wounded, Lt. Neilson, one Sergeant killed, (Sergt T. Berry) and seven other Ranks wounded, some of these casualties occurring on the second day. The Ayrshire and Lanarkshire Yeomanry, who gave valuable assistance in the attack, lost two other Ranks killed and one Officer and three other Ranks wounded. Corpl. J. Priestly 2/1st Lowland Field Co. R.E. who rendered valuable assistance was killed on the afternoon of the 15th.

The shelling, during the whole attack, and especially during the night, was intense over the whole front and along Krithia Nullah. On the right of the East Krithia Nullah the Scottish Rifles Battalion also made a splendid advance, gaining all their objectives which were made good. After their two days' counter-attacking the Turks accepted the situation, when bombing and sniping again occupied our attention. Nothing further marked our stay in the line on that occasion, and the Battalion was relieved by the 5th King's Own Scottish Borderers and returned to Rest Camp in Divisional Reserve.

Captain J.B. Greenshields was awarded the M.C. for his fine performance, and Lt. J.A. Neilson 1/1st Ayrshire Yeomanry and Sergt. T. Berry were mentioned in Dispatches.

SECTION IV.

Dec. 1915

Towards the end of November Winter conditions on the Peninsula of Gallipoli began to show themselves. No sooner were the men in occupation of their Winter dug-outs than heavy rains flooded the ground. Presently the temperature fell, and sleet and snow were followed by severe frost. The Battalion next moved up to the Trenches between the "Vineyard" and Achi Baba Nullah in a blinding snow-storm. Movement in the miles of narrow communication trenches was rendered unusually difficult by the new conditions, as the trenches continued to collect mud and water, and no duck boards were available. A spell of hard frost gave some respite from these minor troubles, which reappeared when the thaw set in, and one had to walk knee-deep in mud through many of the trenches. There was very little fighting at this period, and time was occupied mainly with the upkeep of the trenches. On 30th November Lt. F.J. Cook 10th Border Regt. attached 1/4th Royal Scots, was killed by a sniper. In the first week of December the Battalion returned to Eski Line in Divisional Reserve, being relieved by the 1/1st Lanarkshire Yeomanry. Here Lt. C.B.J. Lancaster (1/8th H.L.I.) and a draft of 40 other Ranks arrived for the Battalion. Major E.S. Girdwood, Brigade Major, was promoted Brevet Lt. Col. and went to Salonica, being succeeded by Capt. W.H. Diggle, Grenadier Guards. At this juncture began a great change in the quality and calibre of the enemy's high explosive shells. This was, no doubt, the result of the Serbian Retreat from the main Orient Railway Line which opened the way for the transport of guns and ammunition to our Front. In the middle of December the Battalion again moved from Rest Camp to the Line, relieving the 1/6th H.L.I. in the central sub-section. Meanwhile a draft of Officers had arrived, including Lt. J.H. Mitchell., 2nd Lieut. P.R. Meredith, and 2nd Lieut. J.N. Shaw from home. The Battalion took up the position from the junction of trench "Forrest Road" westwards, as well as a portion of the R.N.D. Line. The Turkish trenches were found in places to be little more than a dozen yards from our own, and certain sections of these had not been held owing to the ease with which the enemy could throw over bombs. Our Bombers, however, successfully dealt with the situation, speedily reversing the conditions by driving out the Turks. Lance-Corporal J.P. O'Hara and 1 man were wounded. It was noticed on 20th December that the enemy were strongly manning the trenches on our right as though in preparation for an attack accurate bombing sufficed to scatter his force, which suffered severely. The Battalion was again relieved by the 1/1st Lanarkshire Yeomanry on 22nd Decmeber and moved to the Eski Line in reserve, where a very disagreeable Christmas was spent owing to the weather conditions, afterwards proceeding to Rest Camp on relief by 1/7th H.L.I.. During this period of Krithia Nullah and the Eski Line suffered severely from enemy shell fire which increased in intensity later, when the Battalion on 29th December, moved back to the Line to relieve the Lanarkshire and Ayrshire Yeomanry. On 30th December the enemy scored hits on two company cook-houses which were blown to pieces, with casualties, five killed seven wounded and one missing, and next day the casualties were six wounded, and again on 31st December one shell caused six casualties amongst the rank and file. On New Year's day a further/

Jan. 1916

further portion of the Line was taken over from the Anson Battalion R.N.D. from P7 to Hyde Park Corner and occupied by the Battalion. On the 2nd January Nos. 1 and 2 Companies were moved back into support, the 1/4th Battalion The Royal Scots moving back to Parson's Road and the Redoubt Line, on relief by the Scottish Rifles.

Preparations were now proceeding for the relief of the 8th Army Corps on Gallipoli, by the so called 9th Army Corps but on 6th January it became generally known that evacuation of the whole position was intended. Satisfaction at this news was unconcealed, although eminent authorities considered it an unthinkable proposition. It seemed evident, on account on the intense shell fire which the enemy was able to direct on the British positions, that we could hold on only with heavy loss, while the weather was gradually becoming worse and supplies were being detained in consequencez In spite of fears, freely expressed beforehand, that this operation would entail a loss of 50 per cent of the forces it was carried out with extraordinary success. By Friday 7th January, the main portion of the Gallipoli Army at Helles had been evacuated. Shelling was still very heavy about a mile to the West where we after; wards discovered the Turks had been making an attack on the Staffords, which was repulsed, with heavy loss to the enemy. For the space of a week before evacuation we had at night maintained periods of silence in the hope that the enemy might become accustomed to quiet conditions and fail to surmise that our plan of evacuation was in process of execution. Captain Kermack reported that during the night immediately proceeding the final evacuation he had dispersed a party of Turks who were putting out barbed wire in front of their trench, an indication that they had no knowledge that such precautions would prove unnecessary.

The 156th Brigade had been detailed to cover the final retirement of the 52nd Division, the Brigade consisting of The Royal Scots Battalion, (4th and 7th) the Scottish Rifle Battalion (7th and 8th) along with about 250 Officers and other Ranks of the 6th and 7th Highland Light Infantry and a section of the 1/3rd Kent R.E. all under Brig. Gen. L.C. Koe, Commanding the 156th Infantry Brigade. For the last night the strength of the Garrison holding the front line had been reduced to one man per four yards. Only the stoutest-hearted men had been retained. The rest, with all stores, had, during the previous two nights, been sent off, a certain number being again landed in daylight on the Peninsula to deceive the Turks and give an idea of reinforcements landing rather than of evacuation taking place. Dummy figures were also made and stationed in the trenches and all water-proof sheets forming shelter were left in position to deceive enemy airmen.

Photo

The evacuation started, for the last night, 8th/9th January, 1916 at half past eight o'clock, and was carried through without a hitch. (every man being counted at control points) till the last man had arrived on board a transport. The careful arrangements made for the secrecy of the movement proved entirely successful. A large share of the credit for the successful embarkation of the troops and for their safe transport to the Harbour of/

Mudros is due to the Naval authorities, who, in spite of rising wind and tide, carried out completely the programme laid down.

The majority of the troops of the 156th Brigade embarked on H.M. Battleship "Prince George", which lay for a considerable time in the roadstead, off Seddul Bahr, and came quite often under the enemy search-lights. Notwithstanding this the embarkation of troops was carried on without interuption, although "Asiatic Anne" kept up a continuous shell fire on V. Beach, and the ship sailed shortly after midnight. About 2 o'clock in the morning she was struck by a torpedo from an enemy submarine which luckily failed to explode. The Royal Scots Battalion (4th and 7th Royal Scots) landed at Sarpi Pier, Mudros at 9 a.m., on Sunday 9th January. Major Mitchell, who had remained with a party of one hundred men to guard the Eski Line, left at 2 a.m. 9th January in the T.B.D. "Bulldog" which, owing to rough weather and the presence of the Submarine, made for a nearer Port on Imbros. Some anxiety was caused through their failing to appear, but it was allayed when they rejoined on the Monday afternoon. Next day the Brigadier inspected the Brigade, congratulating all ranks on their splendid behaviour, and handed the following special Order to Lieut. Col. Peebles commanding The Royal Scots Battalion:-

SPECIAL ORDER B.M.820

THE ROYAL SCOTS BATTALION.,
(1/4th and 1/7th Battalions, The Royal Scots)

The G.O.C. 156th Infantry Brigade wishes to express to all Ranks of his Brigade his satisfaction and pleasure with their conduct during the evacuation of Helles.

He fully realises the extra hardships it entailed on The Royal Scots Battalion and Scottish Rifles Battalion owing to prolonged spell of duty in the trenches beforehand.

To the 156th Infantry Brigade was assigned the place of honour to cover the evacuation of the 52nd (Lowland) Division and thanks to the splendid courage, endurance and steady discipline under trying circumstances, the G.O.C. feels that the confidence placed in the 156th Infantry Brigade was not misplaced.

He wishes to thank all Ranks for their hard work careful preparations and wholehearted support, and feels that when next he has to call on his Brigade for special exertion, endurance and self-sacrifice, he will receive the same ready response.

The 52nd (Lowland) Division was evacuated without one single casualty.

This order to be read on parade to all Troops.

(Signed)   W.H. DIGGLE., Capt.
Brigade Major
156th Infy. Brigade.

Lemnos,
    Mudros 10/1/16.

It will thus be seen that the 156th Infantry Brigade was the first to land and the last to leave the Peninsula. Of the Battalions in the Brigade the 7th Royal Scots was the first Unit to land and the Royal Scots Battalion the last to leave.

The day following Major General Hon. H.A. Lawrence, Commanding the 52nd (Lowland) Division, inspected the Camp. Amidst sufficiently Wintry conditions Battalion and Company Parades were carried out for a few days.

Thus ended a campaign that will prove historical. The 7th Royal Scots played a noble part on the Gallipoli Peninsula. Without hesitation they faced heavy sacrifices in Officers and Men, and many Awards for gallantry in the field were won by the Battalion from Leith. Amongst these were:-

The Croix de Guerre,	to	Lt. Col. Jas. Mill V.D., R.A.M.C.
The Military Cross	to	Capt. (now Major) A.J. Wightman
" " "	"	Lieut (now Major) J.B. Greenshields
" " "	"	Lieut (now Brigade Staff Capt.) D.B. Allan.

The Medaille Militaire	to	Sergeant Major Maloney
The Distinguished Conduct Medal	to	Corpl. (now Sergt) Hook
" " " "	"	Corpl. Ferguson,
" " " "	"	Corpl. O'Hara
" " " "	"	Private McIntyre.

Mentioned in Dispatches:-	Lt. Col. W.C. Peebles T.D.
" " "	2nd Lieut. T. McClelland
" " "	Private A. Hind.

SECTION V.

Jan. 1916

On 15th January Lieut. D.B. Allan left for Alexandria with the advance party and baggage of the 52nd Division and two days later the Battalion less sixteen Officers and their Batmen, embarked on the H.M.T. "Hororata" for Alexandria, which was reached on 19th January. The remainder of the Battalion arrived at Alexandria on 21st January, and proceeded to Polygon Camp, Abbassia Cairo. While the Division was there a detachment of Officers and Men of the Battalion was detailed to assist in quelling a distrubance that arose amongst the Egyptian Reservists who were stationed in Barracks near at hand.

Also on the return of Lt. Col. (Hon.Col.) A. Young V.D. from Hospital, the Royal Scots Battalion was again split up, Lt. Col. Young taking over Command of the 1/4th Battalion The Royal Scots.

Feb. 1916.

Training was carried out both at Abbassia and at Ballah, a station on the Suez Canal to which place the Brigade moved in the middle of February. On 18th February 2nd Lt. G.H. Eastwood and T. McLauchlan arrived, and were attached for duty. Here on 21st February Capt. and Adjutant J.G.P. Romanes, The Royal Scots, received the temporary Rank of Major and was awarded the Croix de Chevalier/

Chevalier du Legion d'Honneur for his good work on the Peninsula as Adjutant. He was now appointed to the Command of the 1/7th Scottish Rifles, being succeeded in the Adjutancy of the 1/7th Royal Scots by Lt. U.A. Currie, attached from 8th H.L.I.

Ballah was the first desert Station to which the Brigade was posted where the men had their first experience of a Sandstorm not soon to be forgotten. The fine sand, blowing like a pea soup fog, penetrated everywhere. It was breathed, eaten drunk and filled every pore. Tents pegged down in the ordinary fashion were easily blown over and soon buried in sand; but generally the weather was good and bathing was enjoyed in the Suez Canal on several afternoons.

Mar. 1916

In the month of March the Battalion moved to Kantara, the Station on the Canal next North of Ballah. The name "Kantara" means in Arabic a "Bridge", and this place has probably been for many centuries a Northern Egyptian Frontier Station, taking the place that Pelusium held in still earlier times when the Eastern branch of the Nile traversed what is now the Sandy Desert. A Temple stood at Kantara in the time of Rameses II i.e., about 1300 B.C. and probably a fort was erected in the seventh century B.C., and was there when Pharoh Nicho was King of Egypt. Kantara is now a large and important base of operations: it presents a busy and animated appearance, and may be regarded as the threshold of the desert.

April 1916

During our stay there, Captain E.D.H. Tollemache M.C., Coldstream Guards took over the duties of Brigade Major in succession to Captain W.H. Diggle and Capt. A.O. Cushing assumed temporary duty as Staff captain 156th Brigade. The time was occupied in training and erecting defence works. Suddenly, however, on 23rd April the Battalion was ordered to Hill 40 about four miles from the Canal, - this owing to an attack on Katia and Dueidar by a strong enemy force. Very soon the Battalion was pushed on to the neighbourhood of Pelusium, a distance of twelve miles, or sixteen, from the Canal. This move was the sole occasion on which the Battalion travelled by rail in the wide stretch of country covered by the British Force in its advance from Kantara onwards. At Pelusium the extreme heat by day, and cold at night, without any shelter, were at first very trying, as all had been accustomed for a period to life under canvas. There, also began the difficulty of obtaining water, which was brought up by rail in tanks, and then distributed to the Troops in "Fanatis" (oblong metal tanks holding ten to fifteen gallons of water a piece) carried on camels.

May 1916

The first march across the desert North of Sinai took place on 12th May, the objective being Mahamdyia, (Chabrias) a place situated on the sea shore about three miles North of Romani and twenty-five miles from Port Said. The ten miles trek over soft sand, under a broiling sun, proved an arduous undertaking, and all Ranks were glad to reach their destination. At Mahamdyia an outpost line was taken up and the construction of defence works commenced Here the intense heat conditions of the desert began to be experienced/

June
1916

experienced when the Khamseen (south wind) blew and brought the temperature in the daytime anywhere from 110° to 125° Fahr, in the shade. During the stay at Mahamdyia the Battalion came for a short period under the Command of Lt. Col. D. Darroch,(late 2nd Battalion Argyll and Sutherland Highlanders) who took over from Major W.T. Ewing Lt. Col. Peebles and Major Mitchell being then absent on leave. Here the men were gradually trained to accustom themselves to trekking long distances over the burning yielding sands with a water bottle of water per man per day. No one grew so much inured to the business as to like it, but the experiences of the first weeks on the the sand proved of the greatest importance when heivy calls were afterwards made on the staying powers of the men marching under a scorching sun and burdened with rifle and heavy equipment. Beside the monotonous and continuous work of manning and improving the defences their only excitement during this time was occasioned by periodical visits of enemy 'planes flying at a great altitude and dropping bombs.

In the middle of June Lt. Col. Peebles returned from leave and resumed Command, taking over from Lt. Col. Darroch, who then assumed Command of the 1/4th Royal Scots on Lt. Col. Young proceeding home Lt. Col. E.S. Girdwood, who arrived from Salonica, was promoted Brigadier General, and assumed Command of the Brigade from Brigadier General L.C. Koe.

July
1916

The ordinary routine of duties continued until July when the Battalion returned to Kantara. Here 2nd Lt. C.M. Smart arrived with a draft of 100 other Ranks. The Battalion remained a week before starting for Sidi Bishr, near Alexandria on 17th July to enjoy a week's rest, which was rudely interupted. At 5 o'clock on the morning of 20th July, 1916, the Battalion was urgently recalled, to Kantara from Sid Bishr, near Alexandria on 17th July to enjoy a week's rest, which was rudely interrupted. At 5 o'clock on the morning of 20th July, 1916, the Battalion was urgently recalled to Kantara from Sidi Bishr, and on arrival, proceeded the same evening up the line to Romani, arriving in the early hours of the morning of 21st July. The cause of this hurried move was as follows:-

Up till the 18th July no large Force of Turks had been west of Bir El Mazar, 31 miles from Romani and 25 miles from Katia, at which latter place alone there is a good natural supply of water for any force crossing the Sinai Desert from El Arish to Kantara. On the evening of the 19th, however, aeroplane reconnaissance discovered the advance of a Turkish Force estimated at 9,000 to 10,000 from Mazar to Bir El Abd neighbourhood, thus threatening Katia, and possibly the Canal. Later and fuller information established the fact that this Force was the 3rd Turkish Division, with German and Austrian artillery and machineguns, and Commanded by the German Colonel Kress Von Kressenstein. At first however, it was not clear whether this Commander intended to attack the British position at Romani and Mahamdyia, or to take up such a position himself as to compel our Forces to attack him. Meantime, the Battalion worked hard on digging and wiring and other preparations for defence.
On/

Map

Aug. 1916

On the 27th No. 1. Company, under Lieutenant J.C. Bell, with Lewis Gun Section, took over the outpost line, covering the Camp, of the Anzac mounted Division at Et Maler to set free the mounted troops for their strenuous work of reconnaissance, and No 2 Company (Captain W.T. Ewing) occupied Post 23 to North East of them. The next day half No. 3 Company took up a position North West again of Post 23 between that Post and the Railway line, as an attack by a Turkish Camel Corps on the rear of the Romani line was considered possible. On the night of 3rd August, No. 4 Company was detailed as escort to heavy Guns near Romani Railway Station. At dawn on the 4th the Camp wakened to bursts of rapid fire and shrapnel in the direction of Wellington Ridge, which overlooked the Trenches covering Et. Maler held by No. 1 Company, and it became apparent that the Turk, making a bold throw for fortune, was attacking at last with every weapon in his hand. Long range H.E. Shells began to burst about the dumps at railhead, and German aeroplanes bombed the Camp Areas, endeavouring to throw the defence into confusion. The Post held by No. 3 Company was at 7.30 reinforced by the remainder of the Company, and Battalion Headquarters joined No. 2 Company in Post 23 while the remainder of the 156th Brigade moved to the neighbourhood of the same post what had now become the threatened flank of the defence, for the Australians and New Zealanders, strongly contesting each ridge, were yet being gradually forced back by the superior numbers of the Turkish enveloping movement. About mid-day Battalion Headquarters and No. 2 Company were sent up to fill a gap between the mounted troops, and No. 1 Company, which had suffered some casualties, (including Lieut. J.C. Bell) had moved into position under shrapnel and rifle fire, the Turks, by this time, having established themselves on Wellington Ridge. No. No. 3 Company relieved No. 2 Company in Post 23. The Romani position, however had been skilfully chosen by General the Hon. H.A. Lawrence to tempt the Turks to such an enveloping attack, as they had just involved themselves in, for their left wing, sweeping round the British right from Katib Gannit sand dune to Et. Maler towards the railway by the very measure of its success laid itself open the more in its turn to attack from the West by mounted troops from Duedir and from the North West by Infantry of the 42nd Division who had detrained at Pelusium Station. By 6.30 p.m., this counter attack had retaken Mount Royston west of Wellington Ridge, which was lost about mid-day, and after dark two Battalion of the 156th Brigade, the 7th and 8th Scottish Rifles, established themselves on the Northern edge of Wellington Ridge itself and dug themselves in. From there they advanced in conjunction with the Light Horse at dawn on the 5th and the Turks on the Ridge, shaken by their exertion and the shelling of the previous day without food and without water, threw up the sponge. Over 860 prisoners with rifles, machine guns and a mountain battery surrendered to the 1/8th Scottish Rifles. The Brigade returned to rest, but not so the Battalion. At half-past eleven it was ordered to rendezvous at a point near Katib Gannit with the 155th Brigade to take part in clearing the palm grove of Abu Hamra, an operation which commenced at dawn on the 6th. No resistance was encountered there, and the troops were pushed on in artillery formation to the occupation of Rabah and Katia where the mounted troops had been repulsed on the 5th by the machine/

machine guns of the Turkish rearguard. Though unopposed, the March was an exceptionally trying one:- the day was very hot and water very scarce, - and at night the Battalion took up part of the outpost line covering the bivouac area under orders of Col. A.H. Leggett, D.S.O. of the 1/5th R.S.F., till relieved about 4 a.m., on 7th August and ordered back to Romani. Thus ended its share in the pursuit.

On 14th August the Brigade moved five miles East, and took up an outpost line just West of Er Rabah and Katia covering the new Railway which was now just beyond Katia. 2nd Lieut. T. McClelland took over the adjutancy of the Battalion from 2nd Lieut. U.A. Currie who was then attached to G.H.Q. Intelligence Branch.

Sept
Oct 1916.
After holding this line for a short time the Brigade returned to hold the defence lines from Romani to Mahamdyia where it was occupied till October. On 11th October began the march to Bir-el Abd, a distance of twenty miles. Bir-el Abd lies about half way between the Canal and El Arish, and when the Infantry reached it on 13th October there was a feeling of satisfaction that the work of clearing the enemy from British Territory was well in hand. The route followed by our Desert Force from Kantara to El Arish and beyond it is one of the most ancient highways of the world. From time immemorial it had witnessed the passing of myriads of hosts between the Nile Delta and Palestine, and the long succession of invaders, attracted by the riches of Egypt, had to pass this way. The commissariat problem troubled all alike, and many found it necessary to establish graneries along the way, particularly where water was to be found. This is what was done by the British Forces also. They, moreover, solved the problem of distances, in the only way possible for a modern Army, by laying down a railway line, good roads, and a water pipe line, while troops were kept in front to afford protection to the Engineers and Native Labourers engaged on the work.

The end of October found the Battalion stationed at Ganadil, ten miles beyond Bir-el Abd, and there a fresh outpost line was occupied.

The good work of the 1/7th Battalion The Royal Scots was recognised in the following message to the Commanding Officer from the G.O.C., 156th Infantry Brigade:-

"Will you please convey to all ranks under your Command my high appreciation of the good work carried out by them in the past twenty-four hours. The cheerful spirit in which the work was tackled points to a high standard of esprit de corps of which I think you may well be proud".

(Signed) E.S. Girdwood., Brig. Gen.,
Commanding 156th Infantry Brigade.

Ganadil, 27/10/16.
Egypt

On 29th October Lt. General Sir Archd. Murray K.C.B., C. in C., Egypt visited the Line.

By this time the men had become quite familiarised with the conditions of bivouac life in the desert They had added a wonderful Arab collection to their vocabulary, principally derived from native camel-drivers on whom English, or the Scots dialect, was first tried with varying success. They soon learnt that "Majnum" (from Magnoon) was the equivalent of "Crazy" or "Daft", that "Imshi" meant "Be off", and so on.

Nov. 1916

The British soldier had besides more opportunity than he welcomed of studying, at close quarters, that much maligned beast of burden, the Camel. Its wonderful carrying powers and readiness to go on till it dropped from exhaustion were generally forgotten when one was observed venting its displeasure by picking up a driver to give him a shake. The process of loading camels was often attended with the risk of a bite, and the worst offenders styled by the men "Majnum" required to be muzzled. Occasionally when a Camel about to be loaded broke loose, the methods by which, for a while, it succeeded in holding off its pursuers while chasing men and officers in turn, finally following the Regimental Sergeant Major, kept a whole Battalion in merriment.

While the Battalion was in Camp at Ganadil the Pipe Band, which had been attached to the Reserve Unit at home, arrived on the scene. It was originally the Camelon and District Pipe Band, and enlisted in 1915 with a view to filling up the gap created by the loss of the Battalion Pipers in the Gretna Railway Disaster.

Dec. 1916

The Turks had now evacuated El Mazar, making it possible to advance the railway and pipe line, and at 8.30 a.m. on 1st December the 156th Infantry Brigade again moving off via the Southern Caravan Route reached Abu Tilul at 3.40 p.m., encamping for the night, continuing the march next morning and reaching El Mazar at noon 2nd December. No. 1 and No. 3 Coys 1 Troop Glasgow Yeomanry, Major A.H. Glen Coats and 1 Section 156th Brigade Machine Gun Company under Command of Lt. Col. W.C. Peebles formed the advanced guard. There was nothing to interfere with the carrying out of the scheme of training that was planned here. The only visible signs of the enemy were his occasional aerial bombing raids. Our own aircraft reported a strong enemy position at El Masaid five miles short of El Arish. Brigade, Divisional and Corps exercises were held against a position resembling as far as possible, the enemy line. Preparations for the attack were soon completed, and the advance began at 7.30 a.m., on 20th December. A ten mile march brought our Brigade to Madaan at 2.30 p.m., where it halted for the night. Here the enemy was reported to be evacuating his position at El Masaid, twelve miles off, and instructions were issued to advance next day, 21st December at 12.30 p.m., as it was imperative to go forward in support of the Australians and New Zealanders who were engaged in the pursuit. A delay, with the camel transport and the issue of rations, prevented a start until 5 p.m., when a forced march was made to Meshalfet, reached at 11.45 p.m., and at sunrise the column was again on the march/

march the objective, being El Arish itself. This was perhaps the most trying day's trek our men were ever called upon to do. There was no wind, and the heat was intense the dunes like rolling billows 20 to 50 feet high and the sand very soft. Soon the minaret of the mosque at El Arish appeared to view, and it seemed as though the journey's end was near, but such was the effect of the clear desert air that when the crest of the next dune was reached the minaret seemed no nearer. After several such experiences, all declared the Turk was taking the mosque with him! The last climb was the stiffest of all, but eventually the 156th Brigade, the first infantry to arrive, entered El Arish at 11.40 a.m., on 22nd December. The Battalion then took up an out post line covering the town. During the following night Lieut. G. Pender was placed in charge of and led a convoy of 250 camels laden with water for the Anzacs. These mounted troops, in their rapid pursuit of the enemy, had moved out Eastwards to Maghdaba without waiting for a supply of water. Lieut. Pender was met with an eager welcome. He afterwards received the special thanks of the General Officer Commanding the Australian Mounted Division, and was mentioned in Dispatches. The following honours were conveyed to the Battalion in the same Dispatch by Sir Arch. Murray C. in C, of the Forces in Egypt, dated 8th March 1917 :-

Lt. Col. W.C. Peebles T.D., received the Order of the White Eagle (Fourth Class) with Swords from H.M. The King of Servia.

Major A.M. Mitchell., Capt G.G. Weir. R.S.M. A.E. Watson and A/Sergt. D. Crawford were mentioned in Dispatches, while Company Sergt Major A. Smith received the Serbian Cross of Karageorge, First Class with Swords, and No. 1858 Pte. R. Hamilton the Serbian Silver Medal from His Majesty The King of Servia.

SECTION VI.

Jan. 1917.

In contrast to their previous desert surroundings El Arish seemed to the troops a veritable garden. They eye, accustomed to the monotony of the desert sand and scrub, rested with pleasure on the green of its cultivated plots and palm groves that lined the wadi El Arish. The supply of drinking water was ample; sea bathing was available; the weather, with the exception of a short spell of torrential rain and boisterous wind at Christmas and New Year, was excellent. While resting, football, the favourite recreation, was now able to be played on suitable ground. The stay at El Arish whilst the work of fortification proceeded, extended a little over one month. The Wadi, which reaches the sea a short distance North of the town, is regarded as the geographical boundary between Palestine and the desert. In Scripture it is known as the "River" (or brook) of Egypt. The first settled Camp which the Battalion occupied was in a large palm grove near the wadi mouth. There was little to disturb the troops resting here, except the occasional visits of enemy aircraft. On one memorable occasion, New Year's Day, they interrupted proceedings at a Boxing Competition. A week or so later they came down low at night and after dropping some bombs sprayed the grove with their machine-guns. The only other excitement was caused by the rough weather at New Year which drove a small minesweeper ashore at the wadi mouth during the very early hours of the morning. When daylight came the thrilling work began of rescuing the crew, and the heavy seas and strong cross-current made it no easy business, but all were safely brought ashore.

Feb. 1917.

Towards the end of January, 1917, just a year since landing in Egypt the Battalion moved from the palm grove to a new bivouac area situated to the East of a village named Nekhl Abu Sagal. The Battalion did good work here, laying down wire netting on the soft sand to from roads for the passage of Infantry. At this time Capt. T.A. Franklin took over the duties of Brigade - Major from Capt E.D.H. Tollemache M.C. A further move East brought the Battalion close up to the El Arish defence line where it took part in the work of fortification. During February The Battalion took its place in the working out of practical schemes for training in open warfare. Brig. General A.H. Leggett, D.S.O. R.S.F. now took over Command of the Brigade from Brig. General E.S. Girdwood who was promoted Major General to Command the 74th Division. In March the Brigade proceeded to Sheikh Sowaud, halting for a night 7/8th March at El

Mar. 1917.

Burj on the way. Finally on 25th March it set out on the march that brought the British Forces into enemy territory, when the political boundary of Egypt was crossed at Rafa, a police station on the Frontier marked by a couple of granite columns. These were inspected during the few hours' halt for a rest at Rafa. Then to the tune "The Blue Bonnets over the Border" from the Pipes the march was resumed towards evening. The going was still far from easy, and the sand in places soft and deep. It had grown dark and little could be seen of the changing scenes on the route, though it was possible to make out, in increasing numbers, little patches of cultivated/

cultivated ground and groups of Olive Trees. The dim lights of Khan Yunus which soon appeared ahead were hailed as the signal that the desert journey was at length drawing to an end. There was inky darkness to impede a rapid settling down amid new surroundings, but by midnight the transport was in, and an outpost line covering Khan Yunus and the village Beni Sala and Sheikh Hamuda to the S. and E, was taken up. The troops had passed through the dusty streets and along a road lined by cactus hedges to the North East of the town, and in the morning found great satisfaction gazing on the greenery of varied shades glad to have reached the desert's end at this ancient caravan-serai associated by traditions with Bible story and still showing traces of the Crusaders work. It was from here one of the Chaplains sent the following very interesting letter home:-

"Our first encampment in Palestine, about seven miles across the border, was one of the pleasantest spots that one could desire to see. Near us was a small town with a ruined castle, dating probably from the time of the Crusades, embosomed in groves of palm and orange trees, while the neatly laid out orchards were hedged by great rows of cacti with their fleshy prickly leaves and brilliant yellow flowers. The smaller fields were similarly hedged in, and after the glare of the desert, nothing could have rested and refreshed the eyes more than the groves and fruit gardens and the deep green of the barley, among which many flowers of diverse colours grew. We spent a single night amid these delightful surroundings with the soft dews falling on us as we lay in the open, and in our ears the cry of the jackals disturbed by our invasion of their haunts. The campaign on this Front has had a character of its own. For many months there was no fighting, but day by day the desert railway was being pushed out for the transport of supplies, and by its side a pipe track to bring water to the troops and animals. As the railway advanced stage by stage the troops marched forward. No one who has not had some experience of the conditions of life in the desert can realise the severity of the strain put on the men. To see them trudging through the soft, burning sand, sometimes over a wire road which they themselves had laid to make the going a little easier, carrying rifle and equipment, weighing seventy pounds, with the relentless sun blazing down on the shimmering desert and little water to drink, to see them in Camp sleeping on sand, breathing sand, eating it with every morsel of food, ears and eyes full of it when the Khamseen blows all this, if it does not make campaigning in Egypt the awful and infinitely perilous business which it is on other Fronts, does make it the supreme test of a man's endurance, and yet the men were cheerful. One is amazed at their invincible good spirits, their pluck and determination to carry on".

While here the first attack on Gaza, which was protected by an elaborate system of entrenched works and redoubts stretching in a semi-circle, took place on 27th March. The British Troops came near to carrying these lines, indeed some of them penetrated to the city, but in the end the position was not maintained. It then became necessary to attempt the capture of Gaza by more deliberate/

deliberate methods. On 30th March the 156th Brigade moved up from Khan Yunus to In-Seirat, about five miles West of Gaza, and after more than a fortnight of preparation crossed the Wadi Ghuzzeh on the night of 16th April for the Second Battle of Gaza. The operations thus commenced were to last three days. Three Divisions were attacking the main Turkish position, their order, from the sea landward, being 53rd, 52nd, 54th. A Cavalry Division and Imperial Camel Corps protected the exposed right flank, while General Girdwood's recently formed 74th Division was in general reserve. The principal operation of the 17th was the capture of the advanced Turkish position at Sheikh Abbas and Mansura ridges by the 54th Division and the 157th Brigade of the 52nd, the 155th Brigade making ground on their left. This was carried out without heavy opposition, and the next day was occupied in consolidation of our gains and the preparation of roads, artillery positions, etc. for the next step forward. After dark on the 18th the 156th Brigade which had lain meanwhile dug in just North of the Wadi Ghuzzeh, moved up behind Mansura Ridge whence they were to make their attack. The general plan of attack for 19th April was an advance on the left by the 53rd Division to Samson's Ridge (a commanding knife-edged sandhill held by the Turks for the advantage it gave of observation) in the centre by the 155th Brigade up the ridge formed by Lee's Hill, outpost Hill and Middlesex Hill to Green Hill, by the 156th Brigade from Mansura across some 3000 yards of rolling plain to Green Hill and Ali El Muntar, which latter is the traditional site of Samson's exploit with the gates of Gaza, and on the right by the 54th Division, which, after taking the Turkish trenches between Sheikh Abbas and the Beersheba Road, was to wheel to its left and attack Fryer's Hill and the high ground stretching North from Ali El Muntar. The 156th Brigade was to advance when the Brigade on its left had got sufficiently forward, and at about 8 o'clock the three Battalions in the attacking line, - 8th Scottish Rifles on the left, 4th Royal Scots centre, and 7th Royal Scots on the right - moved forward the objective of the 7th being the centre of Ali El Muntar Hill itself. The Battalion advanced in eight waves, each of a half company extended to about four paces between each man. No. 2 Company under Major Ewing led, followed by No. 1., No. 3 Company and No. 4. Major Mitchell was in command of the firing line and had with him the Battalion Intelligence Officer, Lt. G. Pender in telephone communication with Battalion Headquarters. For a mile or more the advance was carried out successfully, but the 155th Brigade on the left, after gallant fighting and heavy losses, proved unable to maintain their hold on Outpost Hill. The two leading Companies of the 7th Royal Scots were, by this time, under heavy artillery fire from three directions as well as from machine-guns and beginning to suffer heavy losses. The 54th Division on the right had also been completely checked after some initial success, and it became necessary to withdraw the leading Company (No. 4 Co.) slightly from an untenable and exposed position on what afterwards became known as Camel Hill. Soon after this Major Mitchell was hit, Major Ewing taking over the Command of the firing line, and Lieut. Pender was mortally wounded/

wounded. Capts Kermack Weir and Bell, and Lieuts. Innes Evans and Waterson were also wounded, and many N.C.Os. and Men. Nevertheless, the Battalion held to its ground till after dark,& then withdrew somewhat to a better position about 400 yards back where the Company of the 10th London Regiment, 54th Division came in and prolonged the right. Two days later the Battalion was withdrawn to Mansura Ridge where a strong line was entrenched and wired in. The Battalion Reserve Company occupied a position behind the lip of Mansura Ridge and suffered several casualties from heavy enemy howziter shells searching for our batteries. The objective had not been reached, but a new line had been formed from which as a jumping off place the third and final attempt at the capture of Gaza was eventually successful.

The following Officers and other ranks were mentioned in General Sir Archibald Murray's Dispatch:-

Lt. Col. W.C. Peebles T.D.
Major A.M. Mitchell
Major W.T. Ewing
Captain W.R. Kermack
Captain G.G. Weir
Lieut. T. McClelland,
R.S.M. A.E. Watson,
Private W. Flockhart
"   A. McLaughlan
"   W.McNab and
"   G. Melvin

May Oct 1917

The general line of defence from Sheikh Ajlin at the beach along Samson's Ridge, Middlesex Hill, Mansura and Sheikh Abbas Ridges Mendur and Tel el Jimmi, was now dug and wired in. This formed the coastal sector, and the whole of it was shortly taken over by the 52nd Division. Brigades regularly relieved each other on the different sections of the line while preparations were in progress under General Sir. E.H.H. Allenby, G.C.M.G. who now assumed Chief Command in Egypt and Palestine for a third attempt. A great deal of work had to be done in the way od preparing railways, roads, water and other supplies, besides the bridging of the Wadi Guzzeh at different points. On 19th June Major A. Maclaine Mitchell was appointed to the Command of the 1/4th Battalion The Royal Scots and promoted Lieut. Col. 2nd Lt. Wm. M. Cowan was appointed Battalion Intelligence Officer vice Lt. G. Pender died of wounds.

On 23rd June, 1917 the Battalion was issued with Mark VII (S.M.L.E. Mark 3) Rifles in place of the old Mark VI Rifles which were worn out. On July 14th Lieut. J.N. Shaw was appointed acting adjutant vice Capt J. McClelland who was attached to 156th Infantry Brigade Headquarters.

Then a scheme of intensive training was carried out by Brigades and Battalions when in reserve. Towards the end of October Brig. Gen. A.H. Legget D.S.O. Commanding the 156th Infantry Brigade inspected the Units of his Brigade and expressed his satisfaction with the work/

work done and the appearance of all Ranks on parade. He then explained that there would be a heavy call on all Ranks in the forthcoming operations, during the third and final attack on Gaza, but expressed his complete confidence that the Brigade would fully carry out its tasks. This confidence was not misplaced, and the 156th Infantry Brigade carried all its objectives.

SECTION VII.

Oct 1917

On 30th October the Battalion, which at this time numbered 28 Officers and 896 other Ranks, was inspected, along with other Units of the 156th Infantry Brigade, by the G.O.C. 52nd (Lowland) Division. This inspection was memorable for two reasons, — one that it was the first parade in steel shrapnel helmets, and two, that it was the curtain raiser to the subsequent operations. On the evening also of this day the Battalion, at fighting strength moved into a bivouac area in rear of Merioneth Redoubt at Samson's Ridge, the position of the general reserve. The 31st October and 1st November were devoted to the final reconnaisance of routes and of the enemy positions. The Battalion formed the general reserve for the attack on the Gaza Defences with No. 3 Company (Captain J.B. Greenshilds, M.C.) detailed to guard the communications to Umbrella Hill on thr right flank, and No. 1 Company (Capt. J.C. Bell) as a mobile reserve to the 1/4th Royal Scots during the attack on El Arish Redoubt and the "Little Devil" No. 4 Company (Captain A.N. Rogers) was held in a position of readiness to support the 1/7th Cameronians (Scottish Rifles) on Umbrella Hill, if necessary. At 11 p.m. on the night of 1st November, No. 3. Company proceeded to the rendezvous of the 1/7th Cameronians and followed this Unit when it moved forward to attack the position. A heavy hostile barrage came down during the move of this Company to its position between the S.E. corner of Umbrella Hill and the Cairo Road, but it suffered few casualties. Captain J.B. Greenshields M.C. its Commander was hit by a piece of shell but remained on duty. On reaching its position the Comapny at once dug itself in and wired its front. This task was completed at dawn, and it had a good defensive position for the one platoon and four Lewis Guns which formed the day garrison the remainder withdrawing to the old firing line at Sabket Post. Captain J.B. Greenshields was highly complimented on the excellent line reconnoitred and taken up by his Company in the dark. It could not be improved upon when daylight came in. No. 3 Company held its position until the 5th, when it was relieved by the Scottish Rifles and proceeded to the position of General Reserve. In the meantime No. 1 Company had proceeded at 1 a.m. on the 2nd November to the Necklace Trench as Mobile Reserve to the 1/4th Royal Scots. At 5.20 a.m., it received orders to reinforce the 1/4th Royal Scots, now in possession of El Arish Redoubt as the situation there was not quite cleared up. Two platoons, on reaching their objective found the 1/4th Royal Scots being heavily counter-attacked from the "Little Devil" Trench. The attack was successfully repulsed and a Bombing Station organised. The Turks continued/

Nov. 1917.

Nov. 1917.

continued to send Bombing Parties against this Station, but without success. Corpl. A. Forbes, No. 1 Company, showed the utmost coolness and determination in repelling them, for which he was awarded the D.C.M. In the afternoon of the 2nd November No. 4 Company proceeded to Necklace Trench, taking over the duties from No. 1 Company and at 3 a.m. on the 3rd the Battalion relieved the 1/4th Royal Scots in El Arish Redoubt 2nd Lt. J.K. Stewart was wounded by a sniper and died of his wounds.

The Battalion Headquarters were subjected to severe shelling by day and intermittent shelling in salvoes by night. R.S.M. T. Simpson was killed while superintending the issuing of stores from his dump. Corpl. J.E. Trimmer then carried on, and rendered invaluable service in the issue of stores, always attended by grave risk, and for his courage and endurance he was awarded the Military Medal. Sergt. Major Simpson's death was a great loss. He was a keen and efficient soldier. In the Boer War he served with the Volunteer Company sent out by the Battalion and held the Territorial Decoration for long and efficient service. Corpl. A. Arbuckle Aid Post Corporal, had his arm blown off by a shell, and succumbed to his wounds. On the night 3/4th November, Lt. C.L.H. Marburg, was wounded, and on the night of the 4th No. 2 Company (Capt. W.C. McGeachin) relieved No. 1 Company.

At 11.30 a.m. on the 6th the Turks commenced an intense bombardment on El Arish Redoubt, firing shells of all kinds and calibres varying from 5.9 H.E. to "Whizzbangs" One shell hit the Aid Post, blowing to pieces a man who was in it, wounding two stretcher bearers, two runners and the M.O. Lt. R.A. Hosegood who went off with shell shock Another hit a dug-out killing two men, while another landed in the dug-out of the F.O.O. blowing it up and wounding the officer. Private J. Mackay, the only survivor the Aid Post personnel continued to work untiringly and fearlessly dressing the wounded. For his bravery and devotion to duty he was awarded the D.C.M.

No. 2 Company's area also received special attention from the enemy's artillery. The Signal Station was struck wounding two signallers and Captain McGeachin, commanding the Company, and communications were cut. At 5.30 p.m., the bombardment which had continued for six hours, ceased, and at 11 p.m. a patrol went out and found the Ostrich Trench and "Little Devil" evacuated. Further Patrols confirmed this, and it was evident that the enemy had cleared out. This was confirmed at dawn. During this period until 7th November, the Battalion was under the Command of Major W.T. Ewing (in the absence of Lt. Col. Peebles on home leave) and his narratives of the battle is given above. For his splendid handling of the Battalion he received the D.S.O.

At 4.20 a.m. on the 8th November the pursuit began, the Brigade moving along the shore to the Wadi Hesy where an outpost line was taken up about 500 yards from the enemy who had retired to Askalon. The Turks held on till 9 p.m. when they retreated and the march was resumed at 8 a.m. on the 10th, reaching Mejdel at 2 p.m. where bivouacs/

bivouacs were made N.E. of the village.

At 9 p.m. next morning 11th November, the column moved Northward to Esdud, 30 miles from Gaza. On the morning of the 12th the Turks were holding a rearguard position on a ridge covering the village of Burkah and to the East and West of it.

The Brigade attacked at 11 a.m. On the right the 1/4th Royal Scots, on the left the 1/7th Royal Scots supported by the 1/8th Scottish Rifles (Lt. Col. J.M. Findlay) less one Company two Sections 156 M.G. Coy, and C. Battery 264 R.F.A. under Command of Lt. Col Peebles Major W.T. Ewing commanded the Battalion. The advance, with Nos. 2 and 3 Coys leading followed by Nos. 1 and 4 was for 3000 yards across a flat plain broken only by two wadis and swept by shrapnel, rifle and machine-gun fire. The Turkish position occupied two ridges. The first was gained in daylight and consolidated. The second ridge 800 yards in rear, was assaulted by surprise after dark and entrenched during the night. Two machine-guns were captured and several rifles and some prisoners taken, while numerous Turkish dead were buried when passing over the ground next day. Our own casualties were not light, No. 3 Company alone losing over 50% of its strength. To give the Turks no rest it was necessary to push on, and at 10 a.m. 13th November, the advance was continued to Beshit,, but just before reaching this point the column halted, as the 155th Brigade was engaged with the enemy fighting for the villages of El Mughar and Katra. These attacks were entirely successful, and resulted in a haul of 1200 prisoners and rifles and 24 machine-guns. It was here that the Bucks, Yeomanry made a magnificent charge across the flat plain against El Mughar which was a regular Gibraltar standing up precipitously from the level plain. On the 14th the Battalion marched to El Mughar and relieved the 4th and 5th K.O.S.B. Next day its Front was extended East and West to link up with the 157th Brigade at Yebnah and fill a gap between El Mughar and Shameh. The 7th H.L.I. relieved the Battalion at 6 p.m. the next day when it moved into Brigade Reserve S.E. of Mughar.

Nov 1917

Joining the Brigade Column on the morning of the 18 18th the march was continued to Ramleh where a brief halt was made and the advance resumed at 7 p.m. to Ludd where the Brigade halted and lay overnight by the roadside, a night ever to be remembered as no one had any rest. The Turks, having retired to the North followed by the Cavalry, our Division struck inland towards Jerusalem. The Battalion, supported by two sections 156 Machine Gun Coy and 1 Battery 4 5 Howitzers of the 264th Brigade R.F.A. formed the advance guard under Command of Lt. Col Peebles starting at 7.30 a.m. The route led over the hills via the old Roman Road to Berfiliya thence to Beit Likia where an outpost

Photo

line was taken up on the hill tops. The road was in most places a mountain pass all uphill over rocks and boulders covered with loose stones so that the going was very heavy and in many places single file was the only possible formation. The weather became intensely cold and two miserable nights of rain were experienced. The conditions were severely felt, as the men had only what they stood in viz:- Khaki Drill Jackets and Shorts, all blankets, greatcoats/

greatcoats and packs, having been left at Ludd. Resuming the march at 8.30 a.m. on 22nd November up the hill track Biddu was reached in the afternoon, and an outpost line held by Units of the 75th Division taken over. A first glimpse of the outskirts of Jerusalem was now obtainable about 4½ miles to the East. At 12.30 a.m., on the 24th November orders were received that the Brigade would move into position before dawn about two miles northwards to attack the line Nebala to Neby Samwil (Samuel's Tomb) the objective of the 1/7th Royal Scots being Neby Samwil and the forward slopes of the hill on which the mosque stands. No. 1 Company (Capt J.C. Bell) attacked the right flank of the position with No. 2 Company (Capt J.A. Young) in support, while No. 4 Company (Capt A.N. Rogers) attacked the left of the hill with No. 3 Company (Capt. W.R. Kermack) in support. Owing to the want of roads the artillery could not be brought forward, and as the enemy held all the points of vantage and could bring concentrated artillery and machine-gun fire on the position, it was found impossible to make any progress. No. 1 Company only managed to advance about 100 yards when it was held up, suffering many casualties from frontal and enfilade machine-gun and shell fire. An attempt was made to crawl round the Eastern slope of the hill to get below the firebeaten zone, but all who tried were hit. 2nd Lts J.W. Hutchison and J. MacNab were wounded, the former seriously and No. 1 Platoon had only three men left. During the afternoon further heavy casualties were suffered by this Company.

No. 4 Company, under Captain A.N. Rogers made better progress. Advancing past the left of the Mosque a courtyard was reached in front of which was a big flat roofed stone shed. Bombs rifle and machine-gun bullets seemed to come from all quarters, the only exit being through a door-way commanded by enemy machine-guns. Captain Rogers cleared the shed in front and led some men on to the roof to fire down on the enemy behind the garden walls. Enemy Machine-Guns at once opened fire, sweeping the roof, killing Captain Rogers and several of the men. Capt. Malcolm Smith assumed Command and attempted to force a passage on the left so as to turn the enemy's right flank. The only exit was a gap in the wall through which the men rushed and the enemy guarded this point with a machine-gun. Bombing was tried, but the machine-gun was out of range. A Bomb Station was now established to guard the left flank while a party of Bombers, Riflemen, and one Lewis Gun Section made a determined and successful rush through the gap, though at heavy cost, and cleared the Turks from the first wall which was taken and held. However, the position became untenable owing to concentrated and enfilade fire, the Lewis Gun and Team being blown up, and it became necessary to withdraw. This was done; the dead and wounded were collected and taken behind the gap in the wall, which was again held. Two other attempts met with no better success, and orders were received to hold on to the position gained, with the help of two platoons from No. 3 Company and not to push any further. Without heavy artillery support to breach the walls the successful attack by infantry alone, against such obstacles and in the face of such fire, was impossible. The fierce attack this day, however, assisted very materially in the later operations which caused the surrender of Jerusalem to our Forces.

The/

The deaths of Captain Rogers at Neby Samwil and of 2nd Lt. J.W. Hutchison at Kubeibeh were a great blow to the Battalion and to their men by whom they were highly regarded. Captain Rogers, along with the other N.C.Os. and Men of the Battalion were buried below Neby Samwil. Lt. Hutchison along with other comrades who died in the Monastery Ammaus (which made an excellent hospital) and the Brigade Major, Capt. T.A. Franklin were buried in the Cemetery at Kubeibeh adjoining the Monastery. The service was conducted by the Rev. S.H. Semple., C.F. Chaplain to the Battalion, and was attended by the Div. Commander Major-General J. Hill, A.D.C., D.S.O., the Brigade Commander Brig. General A.H. Leggett, D.S.O. the Commanding Officer and other Officers N.C.Os., and men of the Battalion.

At 8 p.m. the Battalion was relieved and moved back to the outpost line at Biddu which was held until 3 a.m. on the morning of the 26th November when the 2/18th London (Irish) Regiment took over, and our march Westwards to the Coast began. Bivouacs were put up at Beit Annan 2½ miles N.W. of Biddu, and a day's rest granted. Next morning the march was resumed at 9.a.m. The mountain track was in places, under enemy fire, and on the column coming into view the road was shelled. Capt. W.R. Kermack and three other ranks were wounded, while several of the Camels were hit. On arrival at Beit Sira, 4½ miles further on, fighting was in progress 1½ miles to the N.E. and a halt was called until the situation was cleared up. Unfortunately it did not clear up, with the result that the Brigade was diverted from its journey to Ramleh and sent to fill a gap in the outpost line N. of Beit Sira. The enemy was successfully held off and on relief by the 6th Iniskillings on the evening of 1st December the Brigade moved to bivouacs 4½ miles S.W. Next morning the march was resumed at 12.30 p.m. to El Kubab about 6½ miles West. There a halt was made for the night, and at 9.30 a.m. on 3rd December the Brigade marched to a camping area two miles N.W. of Ramleh a distance of about ten miles. After a rest of three days a move was made at 2.30 p.m. to Selmeh about 3½ miles East of Jaffa. The Ramleh Jaffa Road was under range of enemy guns and a certain point could not be passed before dark, so that the move became a particularly trying one in the dark across the open, as a heavy rainstorm came on. This was one of the worst nights experienced as the rate of of progress was not equal to one mile an hour. Great difficulty was caused to the transport by its having to cross a deep Wadi. The rain had made the surface of the ground so slippery that the camels could hardly stand more than one toppled and rolled down the banks of the Wadi, baggage and all. The troops reached their bivouac area after nine hours, having covered only a distance of 7 or 8 miles and the camels arrived in the early hours of the morning. In the lashing rain and cold, without great-coats, blankets or shelter of any sort a miserable night was passed.

Dec. 1917

On 8th December the Battalion with One Section 156 Machine Gun Company took over a portion of the outpost line facing Muannis across the river Auja, the first perennial river after the Nile which we had met on our months of trekking. The line extended from the Bridge over the Nahr el Auja (South of Khurbet Hadra) Westwards for 3000 yards to the junction of the Wadi Barideh at the village of Jerisheh.

Jerisheh. The 1/4th Royal Scots continued the line to the sea.

On the evening of 12th December the 7th Cameronians (Scottish Rifles) relieved the Battalion which proceeded to the German Jewish village of Sarona where opportunities of a much needed wash and disinfection after seven weeks' trekking and fighting were greedily taken advantage of.

During the whole of the above period the rations consisted of Bully Beef and Biscuit with Tea and some Jam. Here however, were many fine Orange Groves and the fruit direct from the tree was much appreciated and found to be very beneficial to health.

The severity of the fighting recently experienced may be judged by the casualty list:- 14 Officers and 310 Other Rank

While in Sarona one shell passing through the roof of the aid post wounded the Medical Officer, Lt. G. Gordon, R.A.M.C., the Aid post Corporal and three others Captain P.J. Moir R.A.M.C. who had been Medical Officer with the Battalion from September 1916 to May 1917, rejoined as Medical Officer vice Lt. Gordon

On the 19th December an interesting and memorable ceremony took place at Jaffa when Major General J. Hill A.D.C., D.S.O., Commanding 52nd (Lowland) Division presented medals for gallantry and devotion to duty to the Officers N.C.Os, and Men of the Division. The Officers, N.C.Os, and Men of the 1/7th Battalion, The Royal Scots amongst these were:-

D.S.O. to Major A/Lt.Col. A. Maolaine Mitchell, Commanding 1/4th Royal Scots.,
" " Major W.T. Ewing
M.C. " Captain Malcolm Smith
" " Captain P.J. Moir R.A.M.C. Medical Officer attached to Battalion
" " Captain T. McClelland 1/8th Battalion H.L.I. temporarily attached Headquarters 156th Infantry Brigade
D.C.M. " A/Company Sergt.Major J. Johnstone,
" " Sergeant A. Leighton
" " A/Corporal Mackay
M.M. " Sergeant W. Beaumont attached 156 Infy.Brigade Pioneer Coy.
" " Corporal E.J.C. Trimmer
Owing to being in hospital the following Awards could not be presented:-

M.C. to Captain W.R. Kermack
D.C.M. " Coy.Sergeant Major A. Gibb.,
" " Corporal A. Forbes.
" " Private W. Anderson
M.M. " Private W. Flannigan.,
" " Private J.E. Raeburn
" " Private P. Ramsay.

Arrangements were now speedily pushed forward
for/

for the crossing of the River Auja (Nahr el Auja) and the attack of the enemy's positions on the high ground on the North side, including the village of Sheikh Mu'Annis perched on a hill. The crossing, about 35 yards wide was to be effected by throwing over light pontoon bridges and by canvas rafts holding 15 men each prepared before-hand by the Royal Engineers. The greatest secrecy had to be taken to prevent the enemy discovering our intention, but the 412th Field Company R.E. under Major B.I. Rolling, D.S.O. which had so long been attached to the 156th Infantry Brigade and had done so well in the past, carried out the work with entirely satisfactory results. The material was constructed well behind the Front Line and carried forward by night and hidden in the Orange Groves near the river bank and crossing places.

       The Division attacked on a 3½ mile Front from the mouth of the river Auja Eastwards to and including the enemy defences of Khurbet Hadra, a broad high knoll overlooking the river. The frontage alloted to the 156th Infantry Brigade included the whole of the defences on the high ground surrounding the village of Sheikh Mu'Annis and Slag Farm about ¾ of a mile in extent.

Dec.20th 1917

       The crossing of the river, which began at 8 p.m., proved a difficult and arduous task. Three days prior to the attack the weather entirely broke down and a continuous and heavy rainstorm soon brought the river down in flood overflowing its banks and water logging the ground. On the right of the attack the weather cleared about 6 p.m., and the moon shone through a semi-clouded sky which seemed an ill omen, and there were many misgivings as to the chances of success.

Photo.

       To add to the difficulties no sooner had the troops begun to cross, than one of the bridges gave way to the strain of the strong current, so that the crossing was much delayed and the canvas rafts had to carry the bulk of the troops. These carrying 15 men at a time were filled and hauled forwards and backwards by ropes attached to the banks. In the end fortune favoured the attempt and all got across in safety. The 1/7th Scottish Rifles sent a Bridge Head Party across first to secure the forming up ground on the enemy side, followed by the 1/4th Royal Scots; then the 1/7th Royal Scots, followed by the 1/8th Scottish Rifles. The 1/4th Royal Scots moved first, to attack Slag Heap Farm. By this time the 157th Brigade began their attack on the defences at the sea shore, and the Turks, finding something amiss, began to suspect a crossing and shelled the river and banks. Fortunately all the attacking troops were on the move and inside of the range of the bursting shells. The 1/7th Royal Scots and 1/8th Scottish Rifles moved side by side, and after advancing about ¾ of a mile by compass bearing, the 1/8th Scottish Rifles turned Eastwards to attack the right rear of the enemy's system of redoubts defending the village The 1/7th Royal Scots moved straight on to attack the rear and Eastward Defences, and to prevent any attempt by the enemy to retreat. It was an exciting time moving in the dark on unknown enemy ground, but it was hoped that slipping in, in rear if sufficient surprise could be effected, would so/

would so shake the enemy's morale that he would be quickly overcome. This proved to be the case and by dawn the position was entirely captured and an outpost line, facing North, North East and East beyond the village had been taken up ready for any counter-attack. The Battalion accounted for many Turks killed and wounded. Two officers and twenty-five other ranks were made prisoners.

One fine machine-gun (bearing the Ottoman Arms beautifully engraved upon it, said to have been one of many gifted to the Turks by the German Emperor) and much equipment and ammunition were captured.

Our casualties were extraordinarily light, being one Officer, Captain Malcolm Smith, M.C. and Lance-Corporal J. McRoberts wounded. The 155th Brigade on the right and the 157th on the left were equally successful and the whole line thus pushed forward to a favourable position for a further drive. The position was advanced 1000 yards next day and strengthened, and at 9 a.m. on the morning of the 22nd the whole line again moved to attack and drove the Turks fighting in rearguard actions back for a further $4\frac{1}{2}$ miles. It was a day of real open war-fare on favourable ground and made a magnificient sight. The new position secured Jaffa from long range gun fire, and while bridges were being thrown across the Auja and the Railway advanced towards Ramleh and Ludd, a defence line was dug and strongly wired in. In turn Brigades relieved each other in the line, enjoying a rest in the interval in the German Jewish village of Sarona about $2\frac{1}{4}$ miles North East of Jaffa.

Jan. to March 1918

The London Gazette of 9th January, 1918 contained the following Mentions by General Sir E.H. Allenby K.C B. for conspicuous service in the field:-

Captain A.O. Cushny, M.C., and No. 300213 Drummer M. Lawson.

The stay here was prolonged owing to severe fighting taking place in the Jerusalem District where the rocky and broken ground in the Judean Hills gave the enemy many advantages.

The line from Sheikh Haram at the sea to Sheikh Balluta and Mullebis formed the last position in Palestine held by the 52nd (Lowland) Division which, in the middle of March received orders to prepare for a move to France.

Its work in the near East had been successfully carried out under all conditions of modern war-fare in the face of many difficulties.

The following further Awards were granted to the Battalion, and presented to the recipients by H.R.H. The Duke of Connaught at Sarona:-

D.S.O. to Lt. Col. W.C. Peebles, T.D.
M.M. " Lce.Corpl. J. McRoberts and Private J. Green

The/

The Division embarked at Alexandria and sailed on 9th April arriving at Marseilles on 17th April. No incident of note took place on the voyage. H.M.T. "LEASOWE CASTLE" conveyed the Battalion. This vessel was sunk by submarine on the very next voyage.

April 1918

The Battalion at once entrained, and after a journey of three days and nights arrived at Noyelles, then marched to St. Quentin en-Tourment where billets were taken up. Here training was carried on in attack and defence special attention being paid to the use of gas.

On 25th, April, the Battalion moved to Mametz, and on 8th May marched to Airand entrained for Acq, marching thence to Hill's Camp Neuville-St-Vaast behind Vimy Ridge in reserve to the 155th, Infantry Brigade.

The honours lists of Jan. 1918 contained the following names for distinguished services in Palestine.

Bar to the Distinguished Service Order

12-1-18 Lieut.Colonel A. Maclaine Mitchell D.S.O.
1-1-18   Major W. Turner Ewing D.S.O.

Bar to the Military Cross

1-1-18   Captain T. Mc.Clelland M.C.
         Brigade Major 156th Infantry Brigade.

May 1918

On 13th May Major W. Turner Ewing D.S.O. was promoted Lieut. Colonel and took over Command of The 1/7th Battalion The Royal Scots from Lieut.Col. Peebles D.S.O. T.D. who received another appointment. Lieut.Col. Peebles had then completed 25 years service with the Battalion during eight of which he had been in command:

The London Gazette of June 3rd 1918 contained amongst the Birthday Honours the announcement of a Bar to the D.S.O. for Lieut-Colonel Peebles.

The following pages written by Captain J.N. Shaw M.C. Adjutant to the Battalion give the record of the Unit from this date until the Armistice on November 11th 1918 when fighting ceased.

The achievements recorded and honours won shew that the Battalion maintained its good name for steadiness and devotion to duty in France as on the other battlefields where it had been engaged.

May & June 1918

The Battalion's first tour of duty in the front line in France commenced on the 23rd May, when it relieved the 1/8th Scottish Rifles, and lasted till 2nd June.

At all times during the Summer it was of the greatest importance to obtain information, especially as to which enemy troops were holding the line in front, so during this period as in every other period one of the main features of the trench life was patrolling. Patrols of varying strength usually one N.C.O. and six Privates, or two N.C.Os. and twelve Privates, always under an Officer, proceeded to different parts of No Man's Land each night, obtaining information/

information about certain specific points, the strength of the wire in front of an enemy sap head, the location of a suspected enemy listening post, or lying in wait for any enemy patrol with the object of obtaining prisoners.

In addition to the shelling, both by gas shell and ordinary high explosive shell, which was more or less as anticipated, there was one feature of trench life in France which was cordially hated by every one, this feature being supplied by the rats, which were of vast size and in large numbers, and seemed to consider themselves the proper owners of all dugouts and their contents. Nothing edible was safe from them no matter how carefully hidden and they certainly provided an excellent excuse for any man who was called on to explain a deficiency in his iron ration. An officer's credulity was being strained rather far, however when he was informed that the rats were to be blamed for removing a waterbottle which had been lost.

June 1918

In June the Division was reduced from twelve to nine Battalions in strength, the Junior Battalion accordingly leaving each Brigade. This meant the departure of the 1/8th Scottish Rifles (Lieut. Col. J.M. Finlay D.S.O.) from the 156th Infantry Brigade, of which it had formed a part since the formation of the Brigade in April, 1915. Good wishes from all ranks went with them on joining their new Division.

July 1918

The 52nd (Lowland) Division remained in the same sector until the middle of July, and trench life for the Battalion became a more matter of routine, such names as Mersey Alley, Canada Trench, Victoria Dump and the Lens Arras Road becoming familiar to all. In turn, the three Brigades relieved one another, all reliefs fortunately being able to be carried out in daylight owing to the situation of the high ground of Vimy Ridge. The troops were transported in Motor Lorries from the rest billets to the end of the communication trenches within three miles of the front line. This walk was fully long enough in the excessively warm weather experienced in June, though loads were lightened as much as possible by Battalion exchanging items of Unit Equipment. Packs were not taken to the Line, and the Equipment of all Ranks was cut down to the bare necessities of life.

During this period, No 302909 Corporal P. Crane, the Battalion Scout Corporal was awarded the Military Medal for a daring daylight reconnaissance of the enemy's position of which he brought back a most exhaustive and useful report On the night of 23rd June two prisoners were captured by a patrol of fourteen other Ranks, under Lieut. S.J. Spence after a fight with an enemy patrol in No Man's Land. For their conduct in this operation Lieut. Spence received the Military Cross and No. 28466, Corporal H. Stanley, the Military Medal.

In accordance with orders, the Battalion never went into the Line at full strength, there always being a certain proportion of Officers and other Ranks left behind at a Divisional Camp. These formed, what was known as the nucleus of the Battalion, and were intended, in the event of very serious casualties occurring to the Battalion, to form the basis of the new Battalion. The Commanding Officer and the Second-in-Command, in turn, commanded the Battalion in the Line/

Line, the other being in charge of the nucleus.

The nucleus also first dealt with all reinforcements who joined, these including, during the summer, Capt. W. Hunter Lieut. S.J. Spence, J.C. Mc.Culloch, F.P. Mc.Gillwray, A.S. Miller, 2nd Lieut. T.S. Kilgour and J.P. Traynor with about 250 other ranks.

There was yet another portion of the Battalion known as the "Administrative Headquarters". This was situated at the Battalion Transport Lines, and comprised the Quartermaster, (Capt. J. Robertson) Transport Officer (2nd Lt. J.G. McIntosh) and Assistant Adjutant (2nd Lt. A.E. Watson, succeeded by Lt. J.G. West)., with their respective Staffs. On them lay the responsibility for getting rations and water to the Battalion and arranging details of administrative work to relieve, as far as possible the personnel in the Line.

In an organised Trench Line the arrangements for rations and water were greatly facilitated by the system of light railways laid to within half a mile of the Front Line. Each evening company parties arrived at the dump to meet the Company Quartermaster Sergeants, who came up with the rations on the train, the approach of which was heralded ever so faintly by the beat of the Petrol Engine. In a very few minutes the train was unloaded, the rations were carried off to the Companies, and the train was away again, as dumps were never places to linger in receiving as they did their full share of shelling, owing to the difficulty of making them inconspicuous.

All Summer, training went on continuously, both in and out of the Line, special attention being paid to training for rapidity of action. The Section Commanders in particular, (the Section consists of a leader and six men) were thoroughly trained to take full command of their men, and act as an independent unit. This training was found of the greatest advantage in the subsequent months. One thing which must have caused the enemy a great deal of wonder and discomfort was the vast number of rifle bullets which fell in his lines, as when a Battalion was in the Line, every N.C.O. and man had to fire five rounds a day morning or evening to keep him accustomed to the feel of the rifle; therefore, about "stand to" a continuous hail of lead sailed towards the enemy.

July 1918.

During this period casualties were very light but unfortunately on the 9th July Lieutenant I.M. Molyneaux was severely wounded when on Patrol and died of his wounds at Aubigny. He had served with the Battalion for two and a half years, and was universally and deservedly popular; his loss was greatly felt. Major J.B. Greenshields M.C. and a few other ranks of the Battalion were able to be present at his funeral.

On 1st July the 156th Infantry Brigade was inspected by Field-Marshal H.R.H. The Duke of Connaught at Mont St. Eloy, and he presented Medal Ribbons to certain members of the Brigade who had not previously received them. No. 300739, Private A. McLachlan received the D.C.M. and M.M. and/

and No. 49213, Private C. Harper, received the Meritorious Service Medal. About this time Captains W.F. Harvey W. Robertson and K. Mackenzie joined the Battalion for duty.

The 52nd Division was relieved from the Hericourt Sector on the 21st July by the 8th Division, and went into G.H.Q. Reserve the 1/7th Royal Scots being relieved by the 2nd Devon Regt. The Battalion moved to Mont. St. Eloy preparatory to marching to Bois d'Olhain about ten miles North West. Before moving off on the 22nd July the 156th Infantry Brigade was inspected by Lieut. General Sir Aylmer Hunter Weston K.C.B., D.S.O. the Corps Commander, who addressed the Battalion, special attention being paid to those men who had been on Gallipoli.

On arrival at Bois d'Olhain the Battalion encamped expecting about a fortnight's rest, but six days later found it marching back to the Sector immediately South of the one it had left.

After a night at Ecoivres, the 156th Infantry Brigade relieved the 11th Canadian Brigade in the Oppy Sector, the Battalion going into the Line on 31st July. Nothing of importance occurred during the next fortnight, except that the Division was shown what could happen when an S.O.S. signal was sent up. One morning just before "stand to" an S.O.S. rocket went up from some so far undiscovered source; it was repeated all down the line in accordance with orders being answered immediately by the roar of the artillery which lasted for twenty-five minutes before being stopped. A man was heard to remark that he didn't think the British had enough Guns in France to make such a noise, but it gave him more confidence to find that they had! His was the general conviction.

The next move was on 15th August, when the Battalion was relieved by the 1/4th Gordon Highlanders of the 51st Division, as the 52nd Division was once more going into G.H.Q. Reserve. The relief took place by night and the Battalion moved to Ecurie (No. 2 Company being gas shelled en route) and thence by rail to Savy from where it marched to billets in and around Berles.

Rumours of approaching active operations were now rife and all preparations made to ensure that battle stores were complete. The Battalion was rendered as mobile as possible by surplus stores being sent to a dump at Aubigny. At least ten days were hoped for in which to get ready for action, but these hopes, however, proved to be without foundation, as about 4 p.m. on the 20th August orders were received for the Battalion to be ready to move that night and at 11.45 p.m. the 156th Infantry Brigade set out. The destination of the 1/7th Royal Scots was Berneville which was reached about 6.30 a.m. next day after a very trying march. No information as to the ultimate destination of the Battalion had yet been received and the 21st was spent in rest and making final preparations for battle. The night's sleep was seriously disturbed, as, taking advantage of a very bright moon, enemy aeroplanes bombed Berneville and its surroundings for several hours. The sight of one of the 'planes coming down in flames partially recompensed the troops for the disturbance. Next morning the 22nd August, about 8 a.m. orders/

orders arrived for the Commanding Officer, the four Company Commanders who were to go into action, and one Subaltern per Company, to proceed at once to Brigade Headquarters and thence to the Line by Motor-Bus. The remainder of the Battalion moved by Motor Lorries at 2 p.m. to Bretencourt, after dumping their packs. It was now known that the Brigade was going into action next day, and the final battle stores having been issued, the Battalion, at fighting strength, 22 Officers and 605 other Ranks, marched off at 8 p.m. to the Brigade Assembly Point near Mercatel where the Officers who had gone ahead, met the Battalion, and the scheme of operations was explained to all Ranks. The march up had been very difficult as the road were blocked with traffic, troops, guns, ammunition limbers, motor lorries, all going up towards the scene of next day's operations.

About 12.30 a.m., the Battalion moved up the communication trenches to the forming up place which was about 200 yards outside our wire. On the way up, the trenches were subjected to a continuous enemy bombardment of mustard gas which caused heavy losses, not so much at the moment as next day, when all who had been splashed with the liquid became covered with large blisters, or became practically blind, being thus rendered quite unfit for further operations. The Battalion formed up in four lines, No. 1 Company (Capt. W. Robertson) being the leading Company, No. 2 Company, (Capt. K. Mackenzie) close up, ready to exploit the success gained by No. 1 Company; No. 4 Company, (Capt. J. Ballantyne) in support and No. 3 Company (Capt. W. Hunter) in Battalion Reserve. Captain J.C. Bell, who was acting as Second in Command, was in charge of the forming up, which was very rapidly and skilfully, accomplished. For his services on this occasion Capt. J.C. Bell later received the Military Cross.

The 156th Brigade was to advance at 5 a.m. on the 23rd August and capture the enemy position in front of Henin, on a front of about 3000 yards to a depth of about 1000 yards. The 1/4th Royal Scots on the right, 1/7th Royal Scots in the centre, and the 1/7th Scottish Rifles on the left. The latter were in position shortly after the 1/7th Royal Scots, but, owing to a delay in the supply of Motor Lorries the 1/4th Royal Scots only got up into position in bare time to move off to the attack at 5 a.m. A splendid barrage supported the attack which was completely successful, and in spite of heavy shelling the Line was maintained. Captures by the Battalion included one Officer, twenty-four other Ranks, three Machine Guns, two Trench Mortars and two **Anti**-Tank Rifles, one of the latter being obtained by an action of great daring by No. 302973, Pte. J. Alexander, and No. 301116, Pte. R.J. Steenson, two of the Battalion Scouts, who each received the Military Medal. (This Rifle has been presented to the Battalion and is now at Headquarters in the Drill Hall, Dalmeny Street, Leith.) Next day a further advance of ¾ of a mile towards the Hinderburg Line was made at 7 a.m., No. 4 Company leading, followed by No. 2 then Nos. 1 and 3 Companys. Little opposition was encountered, and patrols were pushed out to the Hindenburg Line on that day and on the days following to obtain information, an exceptionally good report being rendered by Lt. T.A. Herdman. On the 25th 155th and 157th Brigades passed through the 156th Brigade, and made good a footing/

footing in the Hindenburg Line, whither the 156th Brigade were ordered to proceed on the afternoon of the 26th and to be ready to attack at short notice. With less than an hour's warning the Battalion attacked at 10 a.m., next morning, the 27th August, with the 1/4th Battalion The Royal Scots on the right and the 2nd Canadian Division on the left. The attack, supported by a lifting barrage, was pushed with great vigour and reached a depth of three miles when very heavy machine gun fire near the Sensee River caused a check, and a position was taken up covering the ruins of Fontaine Croisilles. In this advance the Battalion captured two officers (one a Battalion Commander) two hundred and fifty other Ranks, two 77 m.m. Field Guns twenty Machine Guns and unlimited small material. The Regimental Sergeant Major (W.R..Bain) was in charge of the prisoners and thoroughly enjoyed his day.

      The 156th Infantry Brigade was relieved early next day by part of the 2nd Canadian Division and marched back to rest in bivouacs near Mercatel. During five days the Battalion had suffered heavy losses, one Officer, Capt. K. Mackenzie,, and sixteen other Ranks being killed, and eight Officers and three hundred and eighty-eight other Ranks wounded. It was with deep regret the Battalion heard of Capt. Mackenzie's death, as though he had only been with the Unit a short time, he had already proved his sterling worth. The Officers wounded were Captain W. Hunter., Lieuts. T. McLauchlan M.C., J. McNab., J.C. McCulloch., C.A. Cole., S.J. Spence M.C., 2nd Lieuts. J.S. Weir and D. McLennan. All of these recovered, while Captain Hunter remained at duty, being only slightly hit.

      On 31st August, after three days' rest, when 2nd Lieuts. J. Hawthorne and T.S. Sharp joined, the Battalion, under Major J.B. Greenshields, M.C., marched into support to the Battle Line between Bullecourt and Hendecourt.

      The 156th Brigade was ordered on 2nd September to attack the Hindenburg Line at the Southern extremity of the Drocourt Queant Switch, 1/7th Scottish Rifles on the right, 1/4th Royal Scots on the left, 1/7th Royal Scots being in reserve. The leading Units made good their objectives after stiff fighting and 1/7th Royal Scots were ordered to roll up the Hindenburg Support Line to the North of Queant to a depth of eight hundred yards. This attack developed at 8.30 p.m. and as no opposition was met a line was taken up for the night. The enemy was found to be in full retreat, and next morning the 155th and 157th Brigades passed through.

      That afternoon when all were busy clearing up the Battlefield a Motor Car arrived at Brigade Headquarters and greatly to the surprise of everyone Mr. Harry (now Sir Harry) Lauder stepped out. It was announced that he was going to sing a few songs, and speak to the Units, so in a very short time an audience was collected, and where, amongst the barbed wire and shell holes heavy fighting had taken place/

place on the previous day all Ranks were shortly enjoying "Roaming in the Gloaming" and other old favourites. Hearts were somewhat full perhaps, but laughter seemed unrestrained and carefree, - a tribute both to the equanimity of the "Jock" and the power of the famous comedian.

On the 7th September, the Brigade marched to a rest area near St. Leger where it remained for eight days bivouacing under waterproof sheets. During this time endeavours were made to repair the ravages in the Non- Commissioned Ranks, and training was carried on; small drafts also being absorbed.

Captain J.O. Bell, who had acted as Second in Command in action, for some time, left the Battalion on the 12th September to proceed to England for six months' home duty and rest after three years' active service. His place was taken by Captain J. Ballantyne M.C.

On the 14th September, Lieut.-General Sir Charles Ferguson K.C.B. K.C.M.G. M.V.O. D.S.O. the Corps Commander addressed the 156th Infantry Brigade and congratulated them on the part they had played throughout the recent operations, while next day the Divisional Commander, Major General John Hill C.B. D.S.O. presented decorations won during the recent fighting.

In addition to those already mentioned the following Awards were won by the Battalion during the fortnight from 23rd August:-

M.C. Captain J. Ballantyne   Lieut. J.C. McCulloch
BAR to M.M.No. 303019 Cpl. J. McRoberts
M.M. No. 300812, Signaller R. Baird No. 300465, Sig. C. Higgins
    No. 275144 Private H. Kerr., No. 301603 Pte. T. Bryce
    No. 21118, Private A. Fuary., No. 250509 Pte. A. McLeod
    No. 301603 Private H. Grierson, No. 38710 Pte. R. Morri

On the 16th September the Brigade moved up towards the Line once more, and on the 20th the Battalion, under Lt.Col. W.T. Ewing D.S.O., relieved the 5th R.S.F. in the Line on the right of the village of Moeuvres, 1/4th The Royal Scots being on the left and the Guards Division on the right. The Front Line consisted of a series of isolated platoon posts on the forward slope of a ridge, looking down on the dry Canal du Nord. These posts were very shallow and could not be approached by daylight so the relief commenced after dark, and was not completed till 3.30 a.m. From right to left the Companies lay; Nos 2,3,4, Coys each Company having two platoon posts in the Outpost Line, and No 1 Coy being in reserve. By daylight the posts did not seem to be well sited, as any movement was promptly shelled by trench Mortars fired from the Canal Basin, but opportunity to readjust the Line was not offered. About 3 p.m. on the 21st a very heavy enemy barrage was brought down on the whole of the Battalion Area, and especially the Outpost Line. Shortly afterwards it was seen that a very serious enemy attack was threatened and S.O.S. Rockets, were sent up; our artillery promptly answering. All the posts soon found/

found themselves attacked by large numbers of the enemy working up the saps in front and on the flanks with bombs and machine guns. To prevent being cut off all Platoons had to withdraw about a hundred yards where they reformed and at once counter-attacked. Lieut. A.S. Miller with No. 2 Coy. fought his way back to the posts, and then with 2nd Lt. A. E. Watson ably assisted by C.S.M. Fleeting, attacked a Pill Box from which a machine gun was firing. After a struggle this was captured, along with two machine guns, one officer and twelve enemy dead being counted beside the Pill Box.

No. 1 Company, under Capt. W. Robertson who was severely wounded, had repulsed, with heavy loss, a strong and and dangerous enemy attack which after dealing with our Northern Posts, was endeavouring to penetrate between our left and the 1/4th Royal Scots. Under the direction of Capt. J. Ballantyne M.C. the original position was now re-established with the exception of the two Northern Posts, and touch was maintained with both flanks. These two Northen Posts were in a very advanced position and it was found later that they had suffered very heavy losses from bombs shell and machine gun fire. They were finally surrounded and the remainder of the garrison captured after severe fighting. Lieut. A.S. Miller and 2nd Lieut. A.E. Watson were awarded the Military Cross for their gallantry on this occasion, and No. 300164 Sgt. D. Hook who had most ably assisted Captain Robertson received a Bar to the D.C.M.

In this operation the Battalion lost Lieuts. L.Muirhead and T.A. Herdman, 2nd Lieut. R.P. Innes and eleven other Ranks killed Lieut. W.F.R. Macartney and forty-five other Ranks missing (later found to be prisoners, many of whom, including Lieut. Macartney were wounded) Captain W. Robertson and twenty eight other ranks wounded. The three Officers killed were a very great loss to the Battalion, as they were of the finest fighting type and respected by all Ranks. When a further advance was made the Officers and Men were buried together where they had fallen, by the Rev. F.A. Stewart., Chaplain to the Battalion.

After two more days of enemy artillery activity the Battalion was relieved by the 1/4th K.O.S.B. and moved into support to the 155th Infantry Brigade two miles back. On the 26th, however, the Battalion returned getting into position to be in reserve to 156th Infantry Brigade in a general attack next day on the Canal du Nord Line by the 3rd Army. The attack, accompanied by a very heavy barrage, commenced at 5.30 a.m. on the 27th and all the Brigade objectives were made good by the 1/4th Royal Scots and the 1/7th Scottish Rifles, so that the 1/7th Royal Scots merely took up a series of positions in readiness to act if called upon. By the converging nature of the attack the 52nd Division was squeezed out by the Divisions on the flanks, and on the 63rd R.N. Division (old Gallipoli acquaintances) passing through to take up the pursuit of the enemy the 52nd Division was left in the position it had taken and remained there for four days. This general attack had resulted in the taking of the Marcoing Line, East of the Canal de l'Escaut but Cambrai had not yet fallen and the enemy/

enemy was resisting desperately in the outskirts. On the 1st October the 52nd Division relieved the 63rd Division in the Line, the 156th Infantry Brigade being in reserve. Another attempt was made by the 155th Infantry Brigade to force their way into the Faubourg de Paris, a Southern Suburb of Cambrai, but this did not succeed. All Ranks were by now greatly in need of a rest, and on the 5th the 52nd Division was relieved and the Battalion marched next day, via the Bapuame-Cambrai Road, to Boursies, whence, after a night's bivouac, it continued to railhead at Vaux Vraucourt and entrained for Tinoques. This was to be a real rest in billets, and everyone was overjoyed at the prospect. The march from Tinoques to Izel lez Hameau, which was the billeting area, was very fatiguing, but all were settled down by 10 p.m.

There now ensued a very pleasant fortnight's training and recreation, the training largely consisting of short tactical schemes for small Units, route marching and Lewis gun firing. During this time 2nd Lt. A.E. Watson left for six months' rest in England, and 2nd Lts. J.A. Jamieson, J. Kerr, J.W.H. Stewart and J. Cairns joined for duty.

On 19th October the 52nd Division started to march to join the Battle Line of the 8th Corps 1st Army, which, by now, was East of Douai. The route was by Camblain L'Abbe, Souchez, through the old No Man's Land by Givenchy and Mericourt, Billy Montigny to Auby. This march occupied three days.

After two days' rest at Auby a further stage brought the Battalion to Coutiches where two days repairing of roads which had been blown up by enemy mines, was done, before it moved to Lecelles to prepare to take over the Line (for the last time as it proved) from the 5th Berkshire Regiment facing Hergnies on the Jard Canal. This relief was carried out in the evening of the 28th October, and the Battalion held the Outpost Line till the 1st November when it was relieved by the 1/7th Scottish Rifles. At this time Major J. McD. Smith and 2nd Lieut. W. Gibb joined the Battalion from home.

The end was now almost in sight as all Germany's Allies had signed an armistice, but no precautions were relaxed. In the event of the enemy making use of one of the dark nights and slipping away from the line of the Canal, the 1/7th Royal Scots was detailed to cross immediately after the 1/7th Scottish Rifles had made good the East bank of the Canal, and push on after the enemy as quickly as possible, keeping in touch with the cavalry and cyclists who were also to go forward.

On the 8th November about 8.30 a.m. two telegrams were received productive of very different feelings one that the German Plenipotentiaries had received the Terms of an Armistice, and the other to the effect that the enemy had withdrawn during the night and that the action, as already ordered, was to be carried out. Delay was experienced at the Canal as all the bridges had been blown up, but by night a position had been taken up about two miles East of/

of the Canal and touch obtained with the Cyclists, who were four miles ahead. Next morning at 6.15 a.m., the Battalion moved as Advance Guard to the 156th Infantry Brigade, and encountering no opposition made good the line of the Antoing Pommeroeul Canal by 10.30 p.m. an advance of six miles. At Peruwetz and Bonsecours, which were the first inhabited villages treached, the Battalion received a tremendous ovation: The houses were decked with Belgian flags (during the day the frontier between France and Belgium had been crossed), and the inhabitants wished to load everyone with flowers, or give them cups of coffee and cigars; time, however did not permit of all the social conventions being attended to, and the Battalion pushed on to Blaton with all speed.

Next morning, 10th November, the march was resumed, the 1/7th Scottish Rifles forming the Advanced Guard on this occasion and on arrival at Sirault, information was obtained that the enemy was holding the village of Erbaut about four miles away, and that the 1/7th Scottish Rifles were shortly going to clear the village. The 1/7th Royal Scots was ordered up to Herchies a little over a mile from Erbaut to be in support, and a position of readiness was taken up there about 7 p.m. A considerable amount of enemy shelling was going on and owing to the darkness the situation was not cleared up till about midnight, when the 1/7th Scottish Rifles reported Erbaut to be cleared. As the night was very cold two companies of the 1/7th Royal Scots were accordingly put under cover in cottages in Herchies, while the remainder of the Battalion lay outside to await any further orders. During the shelling four other Ranks unfortunately were wounded, of whom one, Corporal Paulin, later died of his wounds, to everyone's regret.

About 9 a.m. on the 11th November the 155th Infantry Brigade began to pass through to take up the pursuit, and about 10 a.m. a wire was received that an Armistice had been signed to come into force at 11 a.m. that day, the text of the message being as follows:- "Hostilities will cease at 1100 today AAA Troops will remain present position pending receipt of further orders AAA Most stringent orders will be issued by Unit Commanders to prevent any attempt at fraternisation AAA Acknowledge AAA Addressed all concerned"

(Signed) H. Sayer Capt
Bde Major 156th Inf. Bde.
1050

Strange though it may appear this announcement failed to raise any excitement probably owing to the fact that the feeling of strain was to take a long time to wear off, and the one idea of all Ranks was to get into billets and have a sound and prolonged sleep. Billets were arranged in Herchies, and for the first time for many months no sound of guns came to disturb the "rest of the weary" that night.

www.ingramcontent.com/pod-product-compliance
Lightning Source LLC
Chambersburg PA
CBHW081508090426
42743CB00015B/3139